Blessed to be a Blessing

The Story of Peter Thiessen
A Remarkable Businessman Who Discovered

How to do Business God's Way
As told to Peter Enns

Blessed to be a Blessing

ISBN 0-943593-89-0

www.peterthiessen.com

www.goodwordinternational.com

Cover Design by Steve Clark
Superior Graphix Inc.

Text Design Consultant: Lisa Simpson
www.simpsonproductions.net

All Scriptures are from the KJV Bible unless otherwise stated.

Contents

3

Dedication

This book is dedicated to my friend,
my business partner,
and the gracious mother of our 5 children,
my wife Sara.
Without her help, her prayers
and her faith in God and in me,
the experiences related in this book
would not have been possible to achieve.

— **PETER THIESSEN**

A Special Thanks
To Our Children & Their Families

We have five children; three boys and two girls. They are Peter, Lisa, Jake, Frank and Sarah.

From our oldest son Peter Jr. to our youngest daughter Sarah, all our children have been involved in the various business endeavors we have had, first in Canada, then in the United States.

Throughout the 18 years of building the **PJ TRAILER COMPANY,** each of our children has played an active role. As they got older and married, each of their spouses also got involved in the business.

This included Lisa's husband Pete Zacharias, Jake's wife Judy, Frank's wife Darcy, and Sara's husband, Henry Friesen.

From shop maintenance, to working on the factory floor, as well as being involved in various management positions, each one of our children have played an important and valuable role in the success of our business.

As members of our family, they are also a part of the story in this book. Without their support and input we would not have achieved what we have been able to do in our business.

They knew about our financial losses as well as our profits. They were family, they were employees, as well as our partners. After the sale of **PJ TRAILERS,** we still work together as a family in many of our ongoing business enterprises, in Canada, Mexico and the United States.

Our children and their spouses have given us 11 wonderful grandchildren who are a joy and delight to their grandparents. We continue to pray daily for our children, as well as the special grandchildren they have brought into our lives. We are two grateful and happy parents and very proud grandparents.

— **PETER & SARA THIESSEN**

Honorable Recognition
Key People Who Helped Tell Our Story

It is hard to write a book when you don't read or write. That describes my situation in this project. This is also why my executive administrative assistant, Isaak Dyck, deserves special thanks and recognition.

Isaak has been my eyes. He has made himself available whenever I needed him. Researching and providing accurate data about our business; sending and receiving emails and reading the manuscript pages to me as we received them; "Isaak, you have done a great job."

Before the sale of our **PJ TRAILER COMPANY,** for several years, Isaak Dyck was also a part of our management team. More than being a responsible and trustworthy associate, Isaak and his wife Tina have also become personal friends of our family.

Subsequent to the sale of **PJ TRAILERS**, our family has made several large land purchases in Mexico. Jacobo Thiessen, a nephew and also the former manager of **PJ TRAILERS** in Mexico, is now part of our office management team in Mexico.

Jacobo and his wife Trudy are two of the finest people you will ever meet. "Thank you both for all you do for us from day to day. We are pleased to have you on our team."

Another key player on our team is Frank Loewen. (We call him Pancho) Frank and Anna his wife, and their family live at the ranch in Mexico. Frank is the ranch manager who keeps everything running smoothly.

With a two-way radio in one hand and a cell phone in the other, Pancho is constantly on call to go wherever he is needed. He is able to solve problems before they happen "Frank, we appreciate what you are doing at the ranch and we want to say a big 'thank you' to both you and Anna!"

Then there is Peter Enns. Sara and I can only believe that God brought Peter and his wife Dorothy into our lives. All of us have marveled at how this happened. Too unusual to be an accident, we know that God had a plan and a purpose in it.

The four of us had never met before we began this book project. We discovered that Peter and Dorothy shared our Mennonite background. Early in their marriage, they actually lived in the town of Winkler, in Manitoba, Canada, where we also started several businesses.

They understood our culture and spoke our Low German mother tongue. (Plautdietsch) Lastly, their home was in Tulsa, Oklahoma, and just three hours away from Tigertown, Texas.

Soon we recognized that we also shared common spiritual values and a mutual love for our Lord and Savior. From the first time we met, none of us have ever doubted that our paths crossed by God's design.

Peter Enns is a talented writer as well as a gifted speaker. It has been a pleasure telling and retelling the stories of God's supernatural provision in our business and personal life to Peter for the writing of this book.

Because I do not read or write, the people and experiences mentioned in this book are mostly from my memory. If there is anything in the book that is not accurate or could be hurtful to anyone, I ask for forgiveness even before you read it.

Our underlying purpose in producing this book is to express our thankfulness to God for what he has done in our life. We want our story to glorify the Name of the Lord, by giving testimony to his greatness and goodness.

I am convinced what God has done for us and is still doing today, he wants to do for every one of his children, each in their own way. **To God be the Glory!**

— **Peter Thiessen**

Introduction

By Peter Enns

The first time we met Peter Thiessen we were fascinated! Our mutual friends Bill and Helen Braun, visiting from Winkler, Manitoba Canada, arranged for my wife Dorothy and me to meet with Peter and Sara Thiessen, on an overnight trip to Tigertown, Texas.

As we entered their beautiful large home, across the road from the gigantic **PJ Trailer factory**, we were cordially greeted by Peter and Sara. (**PJ Trailers,** the business they had built, stands as a testimony to the blessing of God.)

Spending the afternoon with these delightful new friends and listening to Peter's stories of struggles and ultimate victories was intriguing. What impressed me most was that Peter was prompt to always acknowledge it was the blessing and favor of God that caused his business to prosper.

Peter talked about how starting with very limited resources, they built a large trailer manufacturing business that had up to 750 employees and produced a trailer every seven minutes. He went on to say that it had recently been purchased by a Texas financial investment group.

Listening to Peter, as he told of his dramatic and fascinating business experiences, and how God had answered their prayers, I blurted out, "Peter, your story needs to be in a book."

With a background both as an author and a publisher, I recognized the value of getting out his inspirational message in book form, for others to read and enjoy.

Then I discovered that Peter Thiessen had little formal education and did not read or write in the English language. With roots in a Mennonite community in Canada, Peter was born in Mexico, and had migrated to Winkler, Manitoba, Canada in 1970.

11

Peter and his family had gone back to Mexico in 1974, but then returned to Canada in 1979. After ten years in Canada, Peter and his family had come to the United States in 1989 and settled in the rural community of Tigertown, Texas. This is also where he ultimately built his world class trailer manufacturing business.

That night after dinner, Peter and I talked some more about the "Book idea" and I discovered there were others, who after hearing his story, had made the same recommendation.

The Braun's and my wife Dorothy and I spent the night at their guest house. The next morning, after a delicious homemade breakfast, we enjoyed a worship service in a local Mennonite church in the area.

As I pondered this most unusual experience, and after listening to Peter's journey of faith in business, I began to wonder, "Does God have a purpose in our meeting Peter and Sara Thiessen beyond establishing a delightful relationship with new friends?"

For much of my adult life I had been involved in speaking to various Christian business organizations. I knew the spiritual impact a businessman like Peter could have, by sharing his story of God's direction and provision.

After several subsequent visits with our new friends, including numerous phone calls and a fact finding trip to Mexico, Peter Thiessen said, "Let's do it."

It is a delight to help Peter Thiessen tell the story of both his challenges and God's blessing in their lives. In the pages that follow, Peter also shares his conviction that God wants to bless us so we can fulfill our purpose in life and in turn, be a blessing to others.

I discovered that although Peter Thiessen does not read or write in English, he does have a thorough knowledge of the Bible. Using a handheld digital solar powered player, he listens to the Low German version of the New Testament on a daily basis, both at home and on his extended trips.

At the time of this writing he has listened to the reading of the entire New Testament, from Matthew through Revelation, forty times, in the past nine months.

I know you will enjoy the exciting adventures that will take you from Mexico to Canada, to Tigertown Texas, in this book titled **Blessed to Be a Blessing**; and as Peter likes to call it; **Doing Business God's Way!**

Note:

Peter Thiessen has expressed his desire to have this book made available in German and possibly in the Spanish language. It is currently also available as an audio book on www.amazon.com as well as at: www.goodwordinternational.com

Blessed to be a Blessing

Discovering How to Do Business God's Way

"Sara, I am not leaving the office today, until I hear from God." When her husband, Peter spoke those words, Sara knew that he was serious. Peter was a man of his word and she knew that he meant what he said.

In 1991 Peter Thiessen had started **PJ TRAILERS,** a utility trailer manufacturing company in Tigertown, Texas. For the past five years his company had seen a dramatic growth. The trailers his company was building were being well received in the market place. Every day new orders were coming in and there was an excitement and anticipation of a bright future within the company.

However, with the growth of the company there was also a big problem. Peter did not have the needed capital to handle the expansion of the business. He had made numerous attempts to get bank financing, but each time without success.

What added to the financial challenge was the fact that in his past business history, Peter had experienced a traumatic business failure. He had confidence in his ability, but still the fear of another business failure lurked in the back of his mind.

Optimistic about the future of the business and with trailer purchase orders in hand, he had made numerous presentations, seeking growth capital. By now he was weary of bankers saying "we'll call you back in a couple of days." He knew full well it was simply a kind way of saying "We can't help you with your financing."

Peter believed in God, but he was also fully aware of his own shortcomings. He knew that he had made some big mistakes and wrong decisions in the past. In his private life he had often talked to God about his failings. He had asked for God's forgiveness and prayed for strength and wisdom daily.

He and his wife Sara had been married for many years and he valued her insight and support. Early in their marriage he had done things that he knew were wrong and had caused her pain. But he had also asked for her forgiveness. Sara knew she was not perfect.

There were also things that she had done that were not right. But they were in love and had forgiven each other. Sometimes Peter had trouble forgiving himself. Did the fact that he had a business failure in his past, hinder God from answering his prayers?

These were the thoughts that were running through his mind on that fateful Wednesday afternoon. Tired of the financial pressures of business, Peter wanted to spend some time alone talking with God and he did not want to be interrupted by anything or anyone.

Sara had gone back to the house and she too was praying; praying that God would give her husband Peter the strength and the wisdom that he needed . . . and "Yes God, please bring in the finances we need for our business."

Praying was a habit for Peter. He began each day with a time of prayer. Today he wanted to talk to God about his business, so the office seemed the right place to do it. Peter dropped to his knees.

That was his favorite position when he prayed. He knew God was up in heaven, but being on his knees in prayer, just seemed like the right thing to do. It made him feel closer to God.

There was a heaviness in his heart and his mind was fighting fear. But at the same time, he still had a spark of faith. He knew that the Bible says "With God, all things are possible." In another place it said, "All things are possible to those who believe." Peter wanted to believe; that is why he was praying.

By now the tears were flowing down Peter's cheeks as he began his earnest conversation with God. "Lord, you know my heart; I have confessed my wrongdoings to you and to my wife. I have tried to make things right with others whose lives I may have wrongly affected. God, you know I am not perfect, but I believe you hear and answer prayer, and today, Father in heaven, I need to hear from you."

As he continued in prayer, Peter said, "Lord I want to give you our **PJ Trailer Company,** but I'd appreciate it if you would let me run it for you. In the future, when we are able to help others in need, I will tell them that it is God's money we are giving away."

Peter knew that God was not deaf or hard of hearing, but still he raised his voice as he continued to talk to God in prayer. By now it was after working hours; his employees had gone home, so he knew he was alone and no one but God was listening to what he was saying.

But then he heard a knock on his office door. "Who could it be?" he wondered. He was sure Sara had gone home and would not have come back to disturb him. As a businessman Peter was always conscious about his personal appearance. He knew he was not in any shape to entertain a visitor so he continued to ignore whoever was out there.

Still the knocking persisted. Getting up from his knees and drying his tear filled eyes, Peter finally went and opened the door and saw a man standing there. "Are you Peter Thiessen?"

the stranger asked. "What were you doing an hour ago?" "I was praying," was Peter's honest response.

The visitor introduced himself to Peter. "I am Pat Bassano, the senior commercial loan officer at our bank in Paris Texas. About an hour ago I was at the bank and I believe God spoke to me. He told me to come and visit you and offer your company the financial services of our bank."

By now the banker (and God) had Peter's full attention. But having experienced repeated rejection at various local banks, he was somewhat skeptical, especially about the part of God actually telling a banker to come to see him at his office. (Peter didn't know God talked to bankers.)

But as the banker and Peter continued their most unusual conversation, Peter began to wonder; could this be God's way of answering the prayer of a desperate businessman? Peter made the decision; he had nothing to hide. God knew the truth about Peter; he would talk openly and honestly to this visitor from the bank.

PJ TRAILERS, the manufacturing company Peter Thiessen had started in 1991, had been doing well. Beginning with just an idea and hard work, by 1995 the company had grossed over $20 million in annual sales. The problem that he had was a shortage of operating capital.

PJ TRAILERS had a small line of credit of $100K at another bank, but it was not enough to handle the dramatic growth in sales the company was experiencing. Peter had gone to various area banks to try to get the operating funds the company needed, but his efforts had been without success.

Part of Peter's problem with banking and communicating with bankers was a personal secret that he hesitated to share with anyone. As he stood there talking to Pat Bassano, he decided from this day on, it would no longer be a secret.

Every banker Peter had visited had been friendly and said they wanted to help him with his business. Peter was a good salesman, but bankers wanted more than a sales pitch; they also needed a written business plan with forecasts, projections and budgets, etc.

Born into a conservative, working class Mennonite family in Mexico, education had not been important to Peter in his early years. Teaching children the alphabet, basic reading skills and how to add, subtract, multiply and divide, was considered an adequate child's education.

"Higher education," was frowned upon by the Church, as being "too worldly." The Catechism and the New & Old Testament from the Bible were the only other text books used in the church school classroom. This very limited schooling was all that Peter Thiessen had ever known.

By the age of 12, at the recommendation of his teacher, Peter had already quit school. He spent most of his time as a young street merchant, working with his father, selling hand tools and other farm related items to the people who lived in his rural community. He may not have known it, but this was valuable business experience he would use in his future years as a businessman.

Peter Thiessen had, and still has a razor sharp mind in solving mathematical problems. In addition, even as a young man, he was gifted with, what he considered common sense. Everything else he knew about finances and business he had learned the hard way, from the school of hard knocks.

Most of the Mennonite people in Mexico were farmers and lived off the land. This was not in Peter's DNA. Although he may not have known the meaning of the word, Peter was an entrepreneur at heart. Where others saw problems, he saw business opportunities. Peter gave a new meaning to the phrase, "Eternal Optimist."

That afternoon, as Peter Thiessen and his new acquaintance began their conversation, Peter decided it was time for him to share his long kept secret. "Mr. Bassano," he began, "I want you to know I do not read or write. That is why I do not have a written business plan to present to bankers."

Pat Bassano just smiled! His immediate response was "Peter, you do the talking and I will do the writing." The banker recognized the special entrepreneurial gift that Peter had, and it went way beyond his very limited education. And besides, this was not business as usual, Pat Bassano knew he was on a divine assignment.

For the next hour the businessman, Peter Thiessen took the banker, Pat Bassano on a guided tour through the trailer manufacturing facility. The banker recognized **PJ TRAILERS** was no small operation and Peter was not a small thinker. He saw acres of finished trailers ready to be shipped.

As a banker, Bassano wondered, "How could a $20 million company survive on a $100K line of credit?" He began to see why Peter Thiessen and **PJ TRAILERS** needed the additional lines of credit Peter had been praying for.

One of the first things the banker explained to Peter was that he was dealing with the wrong bank. Not because the bank was not good, but it was a small bank and did not have the capitalization to finance the needs of a growing business the size of **PJ TRAILERS.**

Bassano could see that there was plenty of collateral and other fixed assets to secure the credit line Peter needed. Another unusual aspect of the company was that all the trailers manufactured were sold on a cash basis. As a result the company had practically no accounts receivable.

As this amazing visit between the businessman and the banker came to a close, Pat Bassano said, "Peter, I will have a bank line of credit in the amount of $1.5 million for you within 72 hours." As the businessman and the banker said "Good Bye," they both knew beyond a shadow of a doubt, that God hears and answers prayers.

When Peter came back to the house, after this dramatic visit with Pat Bassano, Sara could see that something unusual had happened to him. There was a smile on his face that Peter could not hide. The heavy financial burden that he had carried for days had lifted. She knew that God had heard and answered their prayers.

At this point Peter and Sara had been married for over 25 years but they were more than husband and wife; they were friends and partners in life as well as in business. They were a family operation that included their five children as well as the new Company they were building.

Sara was excited! She wanted all the details of the unusual visitor who had come to the office. Who was he and how did he know what they needed? Sometimes a man of few words, Peter glanced heavenward, pointing his index finger to the sky. Both Peter and Sara knew the answer; It was God.

That night as they knelt by their bed, as they did every morning and every night, their hearts were overflowing with thanksgiving to their heavenly Father. Peter and Sara Thiessen both knew that **PJ TRAILERS** now belonged to God. They had made a promise and they intended to keep it.

The next morning Peter was up early. He had the commitment of the banker Pat Bassano, and Peter believed him. But he knew that there could still be more phone calls and questions as well as some documentation that the bank would require before the new line of credit would be available.

There was also a new excitement in the air at the **PJ TRAILER COMPANY**, as Peter shared the good news with some of the key management people. He told them that the line of credit the company had so badly needed would immediately be increased from $100 thousand to $1.5 million!

As a businessman, Peter knew the purchasing power of cash and how it would affect the bottom line of the company. He could hardly wait to get on the phone with his vendors and suppliers to begin negotiating better prices. He knew, now they could write the check for the steel shipments, wheel assemblies, tires and all the other parts used in the process of trailer manufacturing. Peter was ready to do business.

Around noon that day, Peter Thiessen received a call from Mr. Bassano, "Peter, I won't have the line of credit in the 72 hours I promised you." There was a silence on the phone and Peter's mind was spinning. He thought to himself, "I can't believe this phone call is happening to me!" It reminded him of the various other bank turn downs he had experienced.

As a businessman, Peter had learned to make quick decisions. It was a part of his nature, but sometimes it also showed up in his having a rather short temper. He could feel the increase in his heart rate, as he waited for the banker to explain his statement.

Pat Bassano continued, "Peter, if you can make it to the bank before closing time today, we can have your line of credit available to you by tonight." "I'll be there," was Peter's prompt response. As he finished the phone call, he felt embarrassed. "Lord forgive me for doubting you," was all he could say.

Always in a hurry, Peter was glad there were no cops on the winding road as he and Sara drove the 18 miles from Tigertown, to Paris, Texas. When Peter and Sara Thiessen walked into the bank, Pat Bassano had everything ready.

Peter likes to wear a hat. It maybe that it adds to his stature, or simply because he likes the look of a Stetson. In any event, that afternoon, simply out of respect, hat in hand, he and Sara entered the elegant bank boardroom.

Running a trailer manufacturing plant, Peter felt a lot more comfortable on the factory floor, than he did at the bank. As they sat at the formal long table, Pat Bassano went over the terms of the line of credit one more time.

In just a matter of minutes their signatures were on the line. Looking at his watch, Peter realized that within just 23 hours of the time he had prayed and met the banker, Pat Bassano, God had done a miracle. The $1.5 million line of credit they needed was in the Company's bank account.

Mennonites in Mexico

In Search of a New Promised Land

In January of 1921 six Mennonite Church leaders took a long train ride to Mexico from Canada. All six were elders from the Old Colony Mennonite Church in Southern Manitoba and Saskatchewan. This was not a vacation; they were going to Mexico on a specific mission.

They had heard that the President of Mexico was extending an invitation to immigrants who would like to come and settle in Mexico. Interested in his generous offer, they were making an extended tour of the country to further investigate and verify the settlement proposal extended by the Mexican Government.

What made it so appealing to them was the promise that if they moved to Mexico they would be able to live life the way they wanted to live it. There would be no government interference of any kind. This meant they would also be free to set up their own church school system.

What was very important to them; they needed the assurance that their sons would never have to serve in the Mexican military system. Finally, they also wanted to be able to maintain the use of their own unique "Low German" (Plautdietsch) language.

Being a church based group, of course they must have total freedom to practice their faith. These Old Colony Mennonites had lived in Canada, just over 50 years. They had come from Russia as pioneers, under basically the same conditions they were now seeking from the Mexican government.

Before this group had migrated to Canada, the Canadian Government agreed to their terms and conditions. But after just a short 50 years, Canada changed the rules and required every child, including the children of the Mennonites, to attend English speaking public schools.

This was not acceptable to the Mennonite leaders. Canada was not living up to the terms of its agreement. They felt betrayed! But being Mennonites, they were determined not to fight with the government. In their minds they only had one option. They had to find a new homeland where they could settle and live their lives the way they desired to live.

Few places are colder than a January day on the prairies of Canada. Leaving in the middle of a Canadian winter and arriving in the warm climate of Mexico was certainly enjoyable for them. Their trip took them from north to south and east to west, as they crisscrossed the landscape of Mexico.

They saw mountains and valleys, rivers and plains, fruit trees and timber. They knew they were visiting a vast land. Beyond the long train ride where the railroad tracks stopped, they hired local guides who took them on horseback and finally by mules to some of the most remote regions in Mexico.

They wanted to see all that Mexico had to offer. After months of exploration and travel, they arrived in the city of Cuauhtémoc, in the province of Chihuahua.

It was a small Wild West town, with only a train station and a few small adobe huts, inhabited by a handful of native Mexicans.

There they found a large tract of land available for purchase; more than a hundred thousand acres of semi-arid farmland; and at a price of just $8.75 per acre. By Canadian standards it seemed like a good deal. Still, they had no guarantee of the annual rainfall, what crops would grow in this soil, and how much per acre it could produce.

The six men agreed, out of all the other places they had visited in Mexico, this would be the best location to come and settle with their families. Yes, Mexico would become their new home. Their decision was final; but to make it official, they also needed to have the agreement in writing.

Once again they boarded the train and headed west to Mexico City for a scheduled appointment with the President of Mexico. His name was Álvaro Obregón. Arriving in Mexico City, they received a warm reception at the palace and had a productive meeting with the President.

Finally the church delegates began the long journey back to their families in Canada. In their minds, they were going back with good news. They had found a possible new homeland in Mexico. Here they would once again be able to live life in keeping with the dictates of their religion and culture.

Living under the perceived threat of the loss of their religious freedoms in Canada, this planned move to Mexico seemed like good news to the Old Colony Mennonites. The Church leadership had prayed about it, and they trusted the word of the delegates who had made the trip.

Not having to fear the cold Canadian winters also seemed inviting. Word about this planned Mennonite mass migration to Mexico was spreading quickly in the neighboring villages. Soon there were maps of Canada, the United States and Mexico spread out on the kitchen tables.

Mexico seemed like an inviting, warm country, but it also looked like it was many miles away. As winter became spring, they were faced with a very hard decision. Who was really willing to make this dramatic move, to a country where they had never been?

Could they trust a people they had never met? Would the Mexican government keep its word? This was not for the weak at heart, or for the undecided. Within a year, the final decision had been made. The Old Colony Mennonites from Canada were now moving to Mexico.

Across southern Manitoba and parts of Saskatchewan, soon there were farm auction sales signs everywhere. These hardy people were willing to dispose of everything they had. Other than personal possessions, they were selling everything at whatever price the market was willing to pay.

Finally on March 1, 1922, the first group of Old Colony Mennonites boarded the train at Plum Coulee, Manitoba, for a long train ride headed for Mexico. The train was loaded with household goods of every description. Whatever they would need to survive had been carefully packed. Winter clothing was left behind. They would not need them anymore.

As experienced farmers, they knew they would have to bring seed for the crops they were going to plant in Mexico. Of course they would need tractors and other farm implements. Whatever they could possibly load was on the train. There was livestock of every type and description.

They brought cows and bulls, horses and pigs, as well as chickens, ducks and geese. Even family dogs and cats were included. These hardy pioneers had planned ahead. Whatever animals they were going to raise in Mexico; they were also bringing the breeding stock with them.

On this long journey, the cows had to be milked twice each day. (It provided the passengers with a fresh supply of milk.) All the livestock, including chickens, hogs, horses and cattle, had to be fed and watered on a daily basis as well. They certainly were on a working vacation with everyone doing their part.

Crossing the Canadian/US border, the journey began; Minnesota, South Dakota, Nebraska, Kansas and Texas; to finally arrive in the country of Mexico. During the next four years, 36 trains, each with 25-45 cars with its precious cargo would make the same long trip.

The price of this immigration was enormous with each train load costing upwards of $25,000. These folks were not poor, homeless refugees; and they did not come without a sense of direction. They knew what they wanted; they had counted the cost and were willing to pay, whatever the price, even if it meant giving up their life.

About 7,000 people, (approximately 1,000 families) including the very young, as well as some of the very old made the long journey from Canada to Mexico. For many it meant saying "Good bye" to loved ones and aging relatives, knowing they would likely never see them again in this world.

Among this group of Old Colony Mennonites from Manitoba, Canada were Peter and Margareta Thiessen, the grandparents of Peter Thiessen. They were the offspring of the Mennonites who migrated to Canada from Russia just 50 years earlier. Once again their generation was on the move, to a new country. This time it was the country of Mexico.

A bit of history is in order. Menno Simons, a former Catholic priest and a contemporary of Martin Luther, is looked up to as the founder of the Mennonite Church. One of the main doctrinal differences between Martin Luther and Menno Simons was the issue of infant baptism.

Menno Simons insisted that baptism was only for adults who had made a profession of faith in Jesus Christ as Savior. In church history Mennonites are also referred to as "Anabaptists."

The other main issue that the Mennonites insisted on, was abstinence from all military service on the basis of their being "Conscientious Objectors."

In the late 1700s Catherine the Great, the ruler of Russia had acquired a large tract of rich farm land. She needed farmers to come and settle in the steppes of Russia. She welcomed people of all faiths to come as pioneers to homestead in her country.

When the Mennonites, who lived in Prussia, (The vast German empire), heard about her generous invitation, they were interested in migrating to Russia. However, before they accepted her offer, there were certain conditions that the Russian government had to agree to:

1) They needed the promise that they could keep their own faith and lifestyle without government interference.

2) Their young men would never have to bear arms and serve in the military.

3) They would be able to maintain their own schools and keep their own language.

Catherine agreed to their requests and soon many Mennonites came with their families, to start a new life on the plains of Russia.

As long as she was alive, the Russian government honored her word and the Mennonites enjoyed their peaceful life style. But when the government changed hands new leaders forgot about what Catherine the Great had promised them when they first had come into her country.

Soon the government insisted on drafting young Mennonite men into the Russian military. This was a violation of their faith as well as a breach of their agreement. As a result of this action, once again the Mennonites were forced to look for a new homeland.

They had heard about North America, including the vast country of Canada, as being a new land of opportunity where immigrants from Western Europe had come to settle.

In the late 1800s about five thousand Mennonites from Russia sailed to Canada and settled in western Canada, in the provinces of Manitoba and Saskatchewan.

The decision to come and settle in Western Canada once again was based on the understanding that the government of Canada would grant Mennonites the religious freedoms they desired. (This included the right to maintain their Low German language, have their own church schools and of course no participation in military service)

After just 50 years in their new found homeland in Canada, once again the Mennonites were faced with a challenge. The government of Canada had reneged on its previous promise. Canada required every Canadian school age child, including the children of the Mennonites to attend public school and learn the English language.

This was not just a matter of right or wrong, or what was best for the country of Canada. In their minds it was a broken promise, by a government power. They had settled in Canada in good faith, but now Canada was not living up to its promise.

Being a peace loving people, Mennonites would not fight the government. They would simply look for a new country where they could practice their faith. The decision had been made. These Old Colony Mennonites were leaving Canada.

Mexico would become their new home. Canada and Mexico have little in common. One is cold and wet, while the other is hot and semi-arid. But to the land loving, hard working Mennonites, they could adjust to new conditions, as long as they had the freedoms they so desired.

The trip had been hard. Traveling with children is never easy. The added daily task of caring for the livestock, made it even more difficult. After being on the train for almost a week, finally it was time to clear Mexican customs.

There still were more hours on the train, before they reached their final destination. As the steaming locomotive came to its last stop, the hardy travelers from Canada had finally arrived in the province of Chihuahua, in Cuauhtémoc Mexico. Now it was time to begin unloading the train cars.

Imagine the hardship of 200 plus people; men and women, children and infants, arriving with all their belongings packed in railroad cars. This included clothing, household goods, livestock, home building materials as well as tractors and farm equipment.

There were no hotels and no convenience stores and no place to find shelter for the women and children. As they unloaded, they had nothing but the open blue sky overhead. But they were not startled; they had come well prepared.

Quickly the men began erecting the portable tents they had brought. Soon there were fires burning in the cook stoves and meals were being prepared. The tables were setup and spread with an abundance of good food. It was nice to be able to eat, without the jostling of the table they had experienced on the train ride.

To these pioneers, fresh water was of utmost importance. It was a must for their very survival as well as for their livestock. What a relief when they dug shallow wells and found there was plenty of good water. In later years they would discover there was so much water underground, they were even able to irrigate their crops.

This was the month of March; in Canada it was still winter and there was still snow on the ground. In Mexico the temperature was well above freezing. They could sleep outside under the stars and enjoy the cool of the night. No doubt, even the livestock was enjoying the change of climate.

As they went to bed that first night, no doubt there were many prayers of thanksgiving. Thanks to God for a safe trip and for this new home in a strange land called Mexico. Most likely they also asked for strength for tomorrow to face the challenges of this new world where they were planning to settle down.

By the time the next trainload of immigrants arrived, there was a welcome party waiting. Those who had come on the first train had hot food, fresh water and a place to sleep ready for the new arrivals. These were not just individuals coming from Canada; they were a community with a common bond.

They had faith in God as well as faith in each other. As the settlement began to grow, the Church leaders had laid out a plan based on how they had lived in Canada and earlier in Russia. Each colony was a village of sorts. There was a main street with houses built on both sides of the street.

Some of the wealthier Mennonites had brought lumber and other building materials with them on the train. Soon there were small homes being erected in each new village. Of course, one of the first buildings to be erected was the church school house.

The church school was a simple one room building that provided the educational purpose of the entire village. Others began building houses using dirt bricks made of straw and clay. The hand formed bricks were put into a mold and then allowed to dry in the hot sun.

This was a building technique they had brought from Russia. It had worked in Russia, in Canada and once again it was working in Mexico. The family house and the barn for the cattle were often connected, but usually they were not under the same roof.

Each household had an allotted acreage of land on the backside of the dwelling. This was used for gardening, for cattle grazing and some limited agricultural cultivation. Additional farm land nearby was also available for purchase by individual families.

One of the unique features of the Old Colony Mennonite migration to Mexico was the way the legal title to the land purchase was handled. There was only one legal title to the entire 100,000 plus acre tract, purchased in Mexico. It was held in the name of the Old Colony Mennonite Church.

Each member of the Church had an "unofficial" certificate of ownership that could only be transferred with the permission of the Church leadership. This prevented anyone from selling to either a non church member, or any other person considered as undesirable in the local community.

Although the Old Colony Church had a code of nonviolent behavior, they still had a strict set of rules they enforced. This was done through the church, by the bishop and the elders who were in leadership. An action everyone in the Church community feared and wanted to avoid, was the enforcement of Church discipline called "excommunication."

Any church member who willfully violated the rules of the church was subject to this dreadful action. This forbad all church attendance, even at funerals. With the entire church membership being aware of this disciplinary action, it certainly was something every member in good standing wanted to avoid.

Many of the rules for Church excommunication were based more on tradition than on a biblical basis. There was a strong emphasis on avoiding all "appearance of worldliness" in dress code. For men, it meant wearing bib overalls.

Ladies were forbidden to wear trousers or cut their hair, and all women who were part of the church needed to wear a head covering. Another major point of contention was the use of rubber tires on farm equipment. All tractors had to run on steel rims with spikes. Also the ownership of automobiles was strictly prohibited.

Horse drawn buggies could not have rubber on the wheels; even the use of bicycles was forbidden. And of course there were no radios permitted in the home. Excommunication could last for a month or for a lifetime. That was up to the decision of the accused Church member.

To be reinstated into the fellowship of the Church required public repentance. For the accused, this included admission of the wrong doing, asking for forgiveness from the Church leadership, and the promise of not doing it again.

The Old Colony Mennonites were the first to settle in the area of Cuauhtémoc, Mexico. As the word of their achievement spread, in later years there were also other conservative Mennonite church groups from Canada that followed the example of the Old Colony Mennonites and immigrated to Mexico as well.

Change comes slowly in the Mennonite churches, but today many of the Old Colony Church members drive cars and trucks and have some of the most modern farm equipment. But the basic dress code for women has remained in place.

Also, most of the Old Colony Church schools have not changed. They are still one room school buildings with an adult male teacher who likely does not have any formal teacher training. All classes are still taught in the Low German language and the Bible is the main textbook.

Most Mennonite people in Mexico love working on the farm and are model farmers. Their fields are neatly kept and the equipment well maintained. In addition, in the past 30 years, irrigating the semi-arid land has made a dramatic change in the farming methods and the types of crops grown.

Diversified farming today includes cotton fields and pecan trees and apple orchards. Because of the abundant apple crops, The Cuauhtémoc area today is called the "Washington State" of Mexico. Beans and corn are also being raised in abundance.

The Mennonite communities in Mexico today have a thriving dairy industry. Currently there are 23 Mennonite owned cheese factories in the state of Chihuahua and "Caso Mennonita" is a relished brand of cheese, found on many Mexican tables nationwide. Milk and other related dairy products are also in demand nationally.

With the passing of the years, many Mennonites of necessity have gone into various manufacturing businesses and other related industries. This includes the production of windows and doors, farm equipment, welding and repair shops and yes, even a division of **PJ TRAILERS,** the company Peter Thiessen started in Tigertown, Texas.

Cuauhtémoc, this small Wild West town that had less than a dozen occupants when the first Mennonites unloaded the first train, is now a booming city of 90,000 residents, made up of mostly Mexicans and native Indian population. (Few if any Mennonites live in the city.)

North of the city of Cuauhtémoc, along the busy highway, stands a tall bronze statue of a Mennonite farmer, with a sickle in his hand. It was placed there in 1985, by the state of Chihuahua, to honor the contribution the Mennonite farmers have made to the economy of Mexico.

Continuing down the busy highway, toward the Mennonite Villages, there is a twenty eight mile stretch of road. On either side are some of the best businesses to be found anywhere in Mexico. The majority of them were started and are owned by the grandchildren of the hardy pioneers who came to Mexico from Canada in the 1920s.

Looking out over the lights of the city of Cuauhtémoc at night is a beautiful sight. In the distance, as far as the eye can see, are the lit up villages of the Mennonites, who came here from Canada almost 100 years ago to live their lives in peace and practice their religious freedoms.

This is where Peter Thiessen and his wife Sara and several of their children were born and spent their early years. Here Peter and Sara learned perseverance through good times and bad. No doubt, God had a plan and a purpose for their lives, even before they knew they could have a personal relationship with their heavenly Father.

The School of Hard Knocks
And Papa was the Teacher

Like all the other boys in the village, Peter attended the Old Colony Mennonite Church school. Peter was inquisitive and enjoyed learning. But one day his teacher said, "Peter you are too curious. I think you should stay home and help your father."

With that recommendation, the young pre-teenager, dropped out of school. Like most everyone else in the community, Peter's father Jake Thiessen was a farmer but he was also a businessman. Buying used farm equipment in the United States, importing it into Mexico and selling it to the Mennonite farmers, he had a profitable operation going.

Doing business seemed to come naturally to Peter's father. Jake Thiessen had an entrepreneurial spirit that seemed to be in the family DNA. Without any intention, he was passing it on to his son and Peter was a fast learner. With his businessman father as the teacher, the market place became Peter's classroom.

At an early age, Peter Thiessen discovered that like his father, he too had the ability to sell. Peter enjoyed meeting new people and it seemed they enjoyed meeting him as well. He discovered that if they liked him, they would also buy the products he was selling.

Watching his father, Peter was quickly learning what it meant to make a profit on the sale of his products. As a youngster, Peter's first assignment was cleaning the used farm equipment his father brought in from the United States.

To keep his curious son occupied, his father helped him set up a display of hand tools to sell to customers. In his street vendor booth he had tools of every description, including wrenches, hammers, pliers, chisels and other household wares. Peter felt like he was in business for himself.

At the end of each day, his father checked Peter's inventory as well as his cash receipts to make sure everything balanced. Peter didn't know it, but he was already learning about profit and loss and the importance of keeping good business inventory records.

Peter was good with arithmetic. Adding and subtracting, multiplying and dividing came easy to him. He knew which were the most profitable items to have in his inventory and what were the best selling items in "his store." These were valuable business lessons he would apply later on in life, as he started and developed his own businesses.

In fall, during the harvest season, Peter and his family had another business. They were busy selling fresh vegetables to other households in the villages. Watermelons, corn and fresh fruit were on the wagon as they pulled it up and down the dusty street.

They were food vendors without a license. Once again, each sale they made, meant they were making a profit for the Thiessen household. Even as a boy, Peter knew the value and the power of money. He purposed that he would always have cash in his pocket.

Peter was the grandson of Peter and Margareta Thiessen. They had been a part of the 1922 Mennonite migration from Canada to Mexico. Peter's father Jake, still just a lad of 16 at the time, had come with his parents, not by his choice, but as part of the family.

Like everyone else in the migrant Mennonite community, when they arrived in Mexico, Peter's grandparents Peter and Margareta Thiessen had selected their homestead. Here they would build a home, raise their children and work the land to provide for the physical needs of their family.

It was customary for young adult Mennonites to marry in their late teens and early 20s. This was not the case with Peter's father Jake. When he was past 30 and still not married, his parents wondered, "Will Jake ever find a wife?"

At the ripe age of 35 Jake Thiessen finally found the woman who would mother his children and be his wife for the next 30 years. Her name was Aganetha Hildebrandt. She was still in her teens when she and Jake began dating.

When Aganetha was just 20 years of age, she and Jake were married. Without a doubt, her father and mother had some concerns about their daughter marrying an older man. But then, they also had the assurance that being older, he would likely be a good provider for his family.

Marrying somewhat late in his life, Jake and Aganetha lost no time in raising a family. It seemed that most every year another baby was born. Peter was the second child born into the family. In the years that followed, there would be seven more babies born to Jake and Aganetha.

They lived in a farming community, but in his heart, Jake Thiessen was not a farmer. He preferred the excitement of doing business. Farmers could only reap one crop each year, but as a businessman he could make a profit each time he sold a piece of equipment and Jake liked that.

Although the Thiessen family had come to Mexico as part of a religious church community, on most Sundays, they did not participate in the regular weekly church services. Although each village had its own school, there was only one church for about every five villages.

To some of the villages it meant that the local church was up to ten miles away. Getting ready for church for a farm family required getting up before the crack of dawn to milk the cows and do the necessary chores. Then it could be an hour long horse and buggy ride to get to church and another hour to return home.

Because of this inconvenience, many families simply observed Sunday as a day off from work without any formal church services. Still, in the Mennonite tradition, it was also a day to dress up and perhaps go for a visit to another family in the neighborhood.

Young Mennonite boys were protective of the girls in the village. It was alright for guys from other nearby villages to come and see them, but strangers were definitely not welcome. In spite of this unwritten rule, from time to time, local young Mexicans would come to visit the Mennonite villages. Immediately they were considered to be intruders.

This happened one quiet Sunday morning. Peter and a group of his friends were on horseback, when they spotted a young Mexican stranger hanging around. It was time to show him that he was not welcome. Peter spurred his horse and it took off with a gallop, heading toward the stranger.

What Peter did not see, was the wire clothesline that was strung between two posts. The horse made it underneath the wire, but Peter did not. The wire caught him on the upper part of the chin and cut his lower lip to the bone.

Pulled off the horse, as he hit the ground, Peter could feel the dangling piece of flesh as it hung below the chin. Blood everywhere, he knew this was serious. He would need medical attention, but there was no clinic or hospital nearby.

When word reached Peter's father about the accident, he arranged for Peter to go and see a semi-skilled medical practitioner nearby. When they arrived, the "doctor" took a look. He said, "Yep, this will need stitches." Then he explained that the cut would heal better, if they did not use any anesthetic.

Without a whimper Peter sat through the painful ordeal. Stitch after stitch, the lip was re-attached. There was little sympathy from his father. His only comment was, "That's what happens when you miss church." This was definitely a case of "Don't do as I do, do as I say." You see Peter's father seldom attended any services himself.

Jake Thiessen was a good provider for his family. There was always plenty of food on the table and more than enough clothes to wear. However he had started drinking excessively. In the community where he lived they called him a drunk. This was a bad habit that in his later years, he would find very hard to break.

As young Peter reached his early teens, he began traveling with his father on equipment buying trips to the state of Texas in the United States. In addition to buying equipment, his father also frequented saloons and liquor stores. Being with his father, Peter soon followed his bad example and picked up some of the same undesirable behavior.

In the Old Colony Mennonite Church, all alcoholic beverages were strictly forbidden. Still, privately they were available, even to the under-aged and Peter took advantage of the opportunity. There were known bars and saloons in the nearby town of Cuauhtémoc. It was not uncommon for some of the Mennonite men to quietly slip into town and visit these forbidden establishments.

Peter's mother was the more spiritual parent in the home. She was the one who made sure the children said their prayers at night. Studying the church school Catechism required a lot of memorization. She was also the one who took the time to help each of her children with this important assignment.

Even as a teenager, Peter was a risk taker. He enjoyed a challenge and thrived on doing something new or unusual. Peter recalls the day when he first dared to bring a flask of whiskey into the home.

Being somewhat short of stature, it may have been an effort on his part to establish his manhood. Whatever the reason, it turned out not to be a good idea.

On that particular Sunday afternoon, he was alone in his room in the second story of the house with the whiskey bottle in his hand. There were other young men from the community who were waiting outside for Peter to come and share his forbidden provision with them.

As he came down the stairs, suddenly his mother blocked the stairway. She confronted him about bringing whiskey into the house, but he denied having it. She said, "Peter, you are not leaving the house." Defiantly, he rushed back up stairs and tossed the flask of whiskey to the boys who were standing there below the open bedroom window.

To escape the fury of his mother, Peter made a wild leap out of the second story window. He landed on the ground after about a 12 foot drop. He may have been the hero of the gang, but in his heart, Peter knew that by his actions he had hurt his mother. Things had not been going well between his father and mother and now he was adding to her pain by following in his father's footsteps.

Being in a very conservative Mennonite community, the only mode of transportation was driving a horse and buggy or if you did not own a horse, you could always walk. Even rubber tires on a buggy were prohibited. To the leadership of the church, cars, trucks and tractors with rubber tires were a sign of worldliness and were to be avoided.

This did not sit well with Peter. He knew that some of the church leaders, in their own private lives were not abiding by the very rules they were trying to impose on others. To his way of thinking this was nothing but hypocrisy. Rather than being drawn into the church all the rigid rules and regulations repelled him from joining the church.

"What did rubber tires have to do with God?" Peter wondered. "Why couldn't he ride a bicycle?" "And why was it wrong to use electricity in the home or listen to a radio?" The only answers to his questions were, "The church elders know what is best, and they have said so."

Then there was the issue of dress code for a young man. The church insisted that men, both young and old, wear bib overalls. Peter didn't like the way overalls fit, nor how they looked. Perhaps it was good for farmers, but he saw himself as a businessman. He liked being neat and well dressed. Peter said "No" to bib overalls.

The church elders began looking at Peter as a rebel. With his attitude, they did not want him in church. When he tried to attend, and that wasn't often, he was ignored and treated as an outcast. While the leaders may have had a noble purpose, their methods had the opposite effect. Peter did not need the church and he wanted them to know it.

In the Mennonite community there were no eight hour work days. Work was from sun up to sun down. By the age of 14 most boys were working side by side with other men on the farm. This included Peter, who was small in size, but a fast worker. He was also more ambitious than many of the other young men who lived in the community.

Peter enjoyed Sundays. Not because he wanted to go to church; it was a day off when he could dress up and be with his friends who lived in the villages nearby. As a teenaged young man, naturally his interests also included spending time with girls. Mennonites had large families, so there seemed to be girls everywhere.

Peter never had a problem finding girls he could date. But after a few visits, often when the father of the girl identified Peter's family, he was no longer welcome. His father's reputation as "a drunk," as well as Peter's own public behavior, was beginning to create a problem for him. Rather than change, Peter chose to ignore it.

He knew there were girls living in other villages within horse and buggy driving distance he could visit.

Peter also had another option; he could go to Canada. It was not uncommon for Mennonites from Mexico to visit Canada. Most every family had Canadian relatives, so going to Canada to visit family members was relatively simple. Peter had extra cash available, so it wasn't long until someone offered him a ride.

He was only nineteen years of age and Peter knew he would never get his mother's permission to go to Canada, so he kept his plans a secret. Without telling anyone, on a Sunday morning, when they should have been in church, Peter and his companions left Mexico for a visit to Canada.

Getting a ninety day visitor's visa into the United States was easy and soon the young travelers were on their way. They were headed for Ontario, Canada where Peter's traveling buddies had distant family members. Approaching Canada Customs, north of Detroit, Michigan they had their rehearsed immigration answers ready. "We are going to visit family members in Canada."

When the Canadian Customs Officer asked Peter for the intent of his visit, Peter gave the same canned answer. Asking Peter for the names of his relatives, he was caught red-handed. He did not have any relatives in Ontario, and obviously did not know their names and Peter was denied entrance.

Peter still had cash in his pocket and he made a quick decision. "Take me to the Detroit airport," he told his partners, "I am flying to Los Angeles." Although he spoke little English, he was sure he could find work as a migrant farm worker. With cash reserves dwindling, Peter found himself living in a dingy cheap motel.

One morning as Peter got out of bed he noticed that the sun was rising in the west. At that moment he remembered the words of his mother. "If the sun rises in the west for 3 days in succession, the end of the world has arrived," she had told him. Nothing unusual happened the rest of the day, but he could not get the sun rising in the west out of his mind.

Once again Peter was up early the next morning and sure enough, the sunrise again was in the west. By now he was getting scared. If it happened one more day, he knew it was too late for him. That night as he fell asleep he tried to pray, but he didn't really know what to say. He was away from home, a disobedient young man, concerned he might never see his mother again.

Peter was up before dawn on the third morning. This time he was looking to the east. That is where the sunrise should be. Then he turned around just for a glimpse, and sure enough, on the third day the sun was rising in the west again. He had no option. He had to get back to Mexico, to confess his wrong doing first to his mother and then to God.

By the fourth day, when the sun again rose in the west, he realized what had happened. The sun was still rising in the east; he had simply reversed his sense of direction. Besides being embarrassed, Peter Thiessen had learned an important lesson. When it comes to matters of faith and of the heart, you cannot trust your feelings or your sense of directions.

No where did the Bible say that the world would end if the sun rises in the west for three days. Later in life, Peter would discover the importance of trusting only what God has said in his Word. It was Jesus himself who said, "Heaven and earth shall pass away, but my Word shall never pass away."

Working hard and watching his pennies, Peter was saving his cash to buy another airline ticket and return to his family in Mexico. One day a friend from work came to visit Peter. He noticed the lack of food in the room and asked Peter, "Don't you have any food," "Sure" Peter replied, and proceeded to show him several cans of meat.

On the logo of the can were pictures of two little cats. Not being able to read, this meant nothing to Peter. Politely, his visitor tried to explain to Peter, that those were cans of cat food. Peter knew it was time to increase his standard of living, even if it meant staying in California a little longer.

By the time the California harvest was over, Peter had the funds in hand and was able to purchase his airline ticket and head back home to Mexico. As the airplane took off from the airport runway, Peter wondered if he would ever be back in California.

Just a few months ago he had been excited to leave Mexico. Now he was more excited to be going back home. Although he now had a lot less money in his pocket, he was certainly wiser than when he had left.

Street Smarts

Wisdom Gained from Experience

Having been to California and back, once again Peter's interest was in Mexico and the girls who lived there. His younger brother had been seeing a girl who lived in a neighboring village. She had a younger sister and Peter had heard about her and wanted to meet her.

Although cars were forbidden, his brother had a friend who owned one. He asked his friend to drive to the village where his girl friend lived and invited Peter to join them on the trip. To Peter this was more exciting than a trip to California. At least here he knew east from west.

The girl his brother was dating came from a large family. There were eight boys and four girls. Even by Mennonite standards that was big. As they arrived, Peter could see the house where the family lived and it was rather simple.

But then, he didn't want to own the house; he wanted the girl who lived in the house. When he caught a glimpse of Sara, the younger sister he immediately liked what he saw. Everyone else had already gone inside the house, leaving the driver of the car and Peter alone with Sara.

Peter smiled at her and she smiled back. He asked if she would like to go for a ride to the far end of the village with them and she said, "Yes." Seated next to her in the car, Peter saw how beautiful she really was. As they came to a stop, he took her by the hand and the two of them went for a long walk down the dirt road.

At first Sara was shy, but Peter could see by the expression on her face, she was enjoying his company. This was the first time they had met and Peter wanted to be a gentleman. After all, first impressions are lasting impressions. Peter and Sara were having a wonderful time together and they both knew it.

At the close of the evening they said their, "Good-byes" and they headed for home. This had been a special night and Peter's heart was singing. Not only had Sara liked him, she had also given him an invitation to come back again next Sunday and already he was making plans. This would be a long week for Peter.

There were no telephones in the villages, but still word can travel quickly. Peter wondered, "Would Sara's family hear about Peter's father, the drunk, as well as his own negative image?" At other times, he had not cared much about what people said about him, but this was different. Sara was a prize he did not want to lose.

Sooner or later Peter knew he would have to meet Sara's father. That was when the questions would begin. "Who are you? How old are you? Who is your father? Tell us about your family," and on and on. All week long, Peter prepared himself. He knew he could always talk about his mother. She was the religious one in the family. Maybe, just maybe they would know her family too.

Going to see Sara by car was the exception. Most of the time, Peter had to go by horse and buggy and that was a two hour drive each way. It gave him time to think about himself and his future. He wondered, what would he do for the rest of his life? "Would he always live in Mexico? He had heard about Canada; was it a good place to live?"

It was the third week. This could be the day when he would have his first meeting with Sara's father, Mr. Frank Dyck. Peter didn't pray much in his teenage years, but driving down that dusty country road, he muttered, "God forgive me for all the crazy things that I have done, and please God, help Sara's father to like me."

Peter was a good salesman and he knew how to sell himself. Meeting Sara's parents, Frank and Elizabeth Dyck went well. Of course he was also on his best behavior. If he wanted their daughter, they would need to accept him. On the way home that night, he complimented himself. "They liked me," he chucked to himself, "and I like their daughter Sara."

For Old Colony Mennonites it wasn't wrong to ride in a car. However to own a car or truck was definitely off limits. For the moment, that was alright with Peter. Since he couldn't own a car, he would simply borrow the vehicle and go for a ride. That is what happened on one Sunday afternoon.

Peter's employer owned a small Volkswagen automobile. It was a fun car to drive. He convinced his boss to let him have the car for a Sunday afternoon. Where was Peter going? You guessed it right; he was headed for Sara's house. "This is going to be an enjoyable evening," he thought.

The Volkswagen was designed for only four passengers, but in Mexico it held several more. Seat belts were not an option and of course Peter was the driver. Sara wanted to sit next to Peter but the car had bucket seats. That didn't matter to Sara; she sat in the middle even if there was no seat cushion.

The car had a stick shift, making it all the more uncomfortable for her. But being close to Peter was worth it. Sara was willing to pay the price.

Driving down the dirt roads in Mexico was a rough and bumpy ride. Sara wondered, "Was Peter making the car sway back and forth so she would have to hold on to him?" What she did know, she was falling in love with Peter.

Sara was quite young but mature for her age and now their thoughts were turning to marriage. Throughout her life, Sara had done without a lot of things. Providing just the basic needs for such a large family was all her father had been able to do. She felt sure that with Peter as her husband, there were better days ahead.

For Old Colony Mennonites, marriage was a process. It meant that first the bride and groom would have to join the church, and that was a problem for Peter. There were just too many "Don'ts" in the church rules and regulation. Peter knew he couldn't live by all the restrictions he was asked to abide by. But then he had a plan.

He would take a trip to Manitoba, Canada, the place of his father's birth. There was an Old Colony Mennonite Church there as well. The Church in Canada was not as conservative and that was good news for Peter. Maybe when he got there, they would accept him as a baptismal candidate and then also allow him to become a member of the church.

In the months preceding his departure from Mexico, Peter worked hard and saved his cash. Because his father was still a Canadian citizen, Peter was able to get his Canadian Passport without any delay. His traveling partners had been to Canada before and assured Peter that it would not be difficult to cross the border at Canada Customs.

It was January of 1970. With all his belongings packed in the car, and with $2,000 cash in his pocket, Peter said "Good bye" to Sara, as well as to his family and friends. Peter Thiessen was going to visit Canada for the first time. It would definitely not be his last.

One of the things Peter noticed was that the farther north they went, the colder it got. By the time they reached South Dakota, the ground was covered with snow. Even the lakes and rivers were frozen sheets of solid ice.

As they neared the Canadian border, Peter began to understand why his grandparents Peter and Margareta Thiessen had left Canada and moved to Mexico. It certainly was easier living at 80 degrees above zero in Mexico, rather than 30 degrees below zero in Canada.

Now it was time to find a job and get a place to live. Raised in a Farming community and around farm equipment, Peter felt right at home in Southern Manitoba.

Like California, Manitoba offered seasonal agricultural jobs for willing workers. Peter was willing to do whatever was available to put food on the table.

Already he was missing Sara. If working long hours would help him bring her to Canada sooner, he was willing to put in the time.

Hello Sara

The Name that Means Little Princess

The eleventh in a family of twelve children, Sara Dyck understood the term, "hand-me-downs." That was the story of her life. From the clothes she wore, to the few toys that she had to enjoy, everything had been used or misused by somebody else before she got it.

Even her few school textbooks showed the markings of previous ownership. None of her sisters or brothers had married when Sara was born, so providing for the basic needs of such a large family was a monumental task for her father.

Don't forget her mother; she had the responsibility of getting the food on the table, four times each day. Families who live on the farm are used to getting up early. Cows and chickens don't need an alarm clock.

Every farm had several roosters who were in competition for the task. At the crack of dawn, they could be heard as their "cock a doodle do's" rang out. That meant it was time to get up; head for the barn and milk the cows. That job could include everyone who was of school age or older. Boys or girls; it made no difference. There was work for everybody.

Sara's family always had a sizeable herd of milk cows, so there was plenty of work for each family member. What many "non-farmer" families may not know, each cow had to be milked twice each day; in the morning and again at night.

Allowing the fresh milk to sit over night, the cream would slowly rise to the top. The following morning the cream was carefully skimmed off the top manually. The next step was to turn the cream into butter using a butter churn. There was always a market for fresh butter.

While dairy products were part of their daily diet, cream was used somewhat sparingly. Add it to the coffee, use it for making gravy and once in a while in a special dessert, but never waste cream. With the large herd of cows, Sara's family always had surplus cream to sell. This added a consistent source of income that the family badly needed.

While most little girls in the village were dressed alike, still having an occasional new dress to wear was every girl's dream, but something that Sara seldom was able to enjoy. Sunday was always a "dress up day." Sara's clothes may not have been new, but at least they were clean.

In the Old Colony Mennonite Church, Sunday school for the children was unheard of. Five days of religious school teaching seemed enough for any child. Giving the youngsters Saturday and Sunday off was logical and made good sense.

By the age of six, most children in the colony were enrolled in the village church school, and Sara was no exception. Each village had its own schoolhouse and they all had a similar design. They were simple one room buildings. The boys sat on one side and the girls on the other.

The school teacher was always an adult male. With 50 to 100 students crowded into one classroom, it took an authority figure just to keep order. Generally the teacher had no formal training. If physical discipline was needed, the teacher had the freedom to use the "rod of correction," without any fear of parental repercussion.

In Sara's days in school, all the classes were taught in the Low German language. Beginning at nine o'clock in the morning, school began with the singing of a song taken from the church hymnal. Then the teacher and the students would pray together in unison and the classes would begin.

The entire Old Colony Mennonite Church school system used four basic textbooks. The first book was the "Fibel." It offered the basics of education; including reading, writing and arithmetic. This was followed with the Church Catechism, The New Testament and finally The Old Testament.

The Catechism was a question and answer book that had a dual purpose. It helped students in advanced reading skills and at the same time taught the basics of the Christian faith. Created by the reformer Martin Luther, and the founder of the Lutheran Church, the Mennonite Catechism has much in common with both the Lutheran and Catholic Catechisms.

The New and Old Testament versions of the Bible used in the church school were also the product of Martin Luther. His translation of the Bible has been considered a classic in the German language, similar to the esteem given to the King James Version of the English Bible.

Generally six years of school education was considered adequate at the village church school, and even that was not mandatory, especially for girls. After all, their basic function as adults would be to marry and have children, and then be the housekeeper for the rest of the family.

Growing up in a rural Mennonite community in Mexico, every child was expected to do their share of productive household chores. This included helping in the maintenance of the family garden. Large families needed large gardens, so there was always enough work for everyone.

Ben Dyck, one of Sara's older brothers had contracted polio when he was about nine months old. Polio was almost unheard of in their quiet little community. There was no known cure for the disease and little hope that Ben would ever be able to run and play, or do much hard work physically in his adult years.

In spite of his handicap, there were still some productive things that Ben was able to do. One of those was to drive a horse and buggy. It was Ben's assignment to make several trips each week to the local feed processing plant and pick up bags of feed supplement to feed to the dairy cows to increase their daily milk production.

Usually Ben did not go alone. He had limited physical strength and needed help to load the bags into the buggy. Still he was the driver and in charge of the operation. On one particular day, Sara and one of her brothers went with Ben to make the pickup. Sara was seated up front with Ben, while her other brother sat in the back on the bagged goods.

The horse responded to Ben's "giddy up," but sometimes a horse can have a mind of its own. A harnessed horse is controlled by the driver using the reins attached to either side of the bridle. This gives the horse the signal to turn to either side, depending on the pull. Pulling hard on both reins, means "stop." Lady, the name of Ben's horse, had another idea.

Suddenly the horse whipped its tail into the air and locked the rein tightly against her hindquarter as she leaped into a gallop. Ben pulled with all his might; but still momentarily the reins were locked in place. Ben's brother who was seated on the bagged inventory went sailing off the backend of the wagon as the horse sped down the street.

Both Ben and Sara were hanging on to their seats, as Ben desperately tried to get the horse under control. Having released its pent up energy, Lady finally slowed down to a trot and Ben was able to bring the horse to a full stop.

Turning the rig around, Ben decided to show Lady who was really the boss. Flicking the reins he again pushed the horse into a gallop. In just moments, they were back to where the load had been dumped. A hard pull on the reins and a commanding "Whoa," told Lady that Ben was in charge.

By the age of fourteen most young boys were already working alongside other adult men in the process of farming. In many ways, working on the farm, was similar to attending a vocational school. Here boys could quickly discover their skills and their likes and dislikes for certain activities.

Frank and Elizabeth Dyck, Sara's mother and father, and their family still lived in the same home where her grandparents had lived when they first came to Mexico. It was a house they literally built with their bare hands. The home was constructed of dirt and straw bricks, dried in the sun, with windows and doors appropriately added.

A small three bedroom house, without running water or other modern conveniences, it is still in use today. After almost a hundred years, the house is lived in by a young family in the village. The "outhouse," the forerunner of the modern bathroom, is still in good repair and used to meet the "necessary needs" of the current residents.

When Sara's grandparents first arrived in Mexico, they had little or no cash. Using what they had, they built a modest house on their allotment of land in the village. There was always a huge garden, chickens for fresh eggs, hogs for meat and dairy cows for milk. In later years, any surplus milk and cream provided cash flow to meet the daily needs of the family.

Sara's family of eight boys and four girls, were all raised on that same small village acreage. They did not own enough land to raise large crops. Instead, they grew all types of vegetables and sold them to other village dwellers in the area. Financially things always seemed tight. Even as a young girl, Sara dreamed of leaving home and starting a life of her own.

One day Sara's father, Frank Dyck, had gone into the nearby city of Cuauhtémoc. There at a local hotel, he met a group of deer hunters from the United States. They were on a hunting expedition. Frank loved to hunt and share the stories of his hunting exploits.

As he talked with them, it became apparent that the visitors had an interest in hiring him as a guide for their deer hunt. He had never done this before, but he knew the lay of the land and where the deer were located. This was an opportunity for some extra cash, so he took them up on the offer. True to his word, they had a successful hunting trip.

Word began to spread and soon other American hunters were calling on Frank and his services as a hunting guide. Almost without knowing it he was starting his own little business. Hunting was something that he really enjoyed and was good at and there was an abundance of deer within 50 miles of the village where he lived. This was a great way to supplement the farm.

Not only were there lots of deer in the area; each season, on their migration route south, the famed Canada geese stopped in Mexico. This was a great goose hunting location. Many of the same deer hunters enjoyed goose hunting as well and came back year after year. To Frank this was another good opportunity to increase the business.

Often after a successful goose hunt, the whole family got involved in the goose cleaning process. The goose feathers would be plucked and kept dry. Goose feathers made excellent pillows that would be sold later to generate additional revenue.

Even the kids helped with the goose cleaning process, as they picked the small goose pin feathers. Then the geese were eviscerated and prepared for the trip back to the United States.

The task of cleaning wild Canada geese was not always pleasant. The odor of goose innards could be smelled on the street, but to the Dyck family it smelled liked cash. As a young girl, Sara had her part in working in this family business.

She was just eight years of age when tragedy struck Sara's family. She had a brother Frank, who by now was in his teens. Like most boys his age, he was full of energy and liked to eat. But in recent days, he had lost his appetite and always seemed thirsty. He had also been losing weight. Still no one seemed to know what was wrong with Frank.

Hospitals were only used for emergencies, and this did not seem to be life threatening, at least not yet. Using available home remedies, for the next couple of months, he was treated at home. It wasn't long before it was evident that Frank was very ill; he needed to go to the hospital in Cuauhtémoc, about 15 miles away.

For the next few weeks, under doctor's care, he was not improving. Then they got the diagnosis; it was Juvenile Diabetes. Diabetes was not uncommon in the community, but it was usually older people who had it and never the young. In Frank's case his pancreas had stopped making insulin and within just a few more days, he had passed away.

It was a sad time in the Frank Dyck household. This was the first death in the immediate family and Sara had lots of questions. Now the funeral preparation had to be made. The Mennonite community did not have a funeral home. The body of the deceased was simply taken to the house, placed on a slab and packed with ice.

The funeral was a simple ceremony conducted at the local church schoolhouse. Like most other services it began with singing, followed by a sermon and a eulogy. The final resting place for Frank Dyck, Jr, was in the cemetery, located on the grounds next to the schoolhouse.

Sara still had six other brothers, but she missed Frank. She wondered, was he in heaven now? He had looked so peaceful at the funeral, was he simply asleep? Would he ever wake up again? From the church school Catechism she remembered something about a resurrection day when the dead would rise again. Maybe she would see Frank again; at least she hoped so.

The Mennonite villages in the Cuauhtémoc area have a high elevation, almost 6,000 feet above sea level. This makes for warm days and cool nights. Sara enjoyed the comfortable evenings and liked spending time outdoors with her father.

In addition to hunting, he also enjoyed fishing. At that time it was legal to catch fish using nets. It was not uncommon to return from the nearby lake with dozens of fresh fish. What they could not eat, they shared with others in the village.

It wasn't only fish that was shared among the villagers. It was common to bring fresh soup or buns to other families, and especially the aged. Sara recalls one day one of her friends from her village was passing her house. She was carrying a container of chicken noodle soup intended for a new mom in the village. She stopped to say hello and chat with Sara for a little while.

The girls decided to sample the soup. It was delicious! Sitting on the grass, they ate spoonful after spoonful. Before they knew it the last bit of the soup was gone. It was hard to believe, but they had finished the entire container. Only after they became adults, were the girls willing to admit what had happened to the soup.

Enter Peter Thiessen. Peter's brother was dating Sara's sister. That is how she had met Peter. He lived in an adjoining village, about two hours away by horse and buggy. The first time she saw him, she was impressed. He had been to the United States and appeared to know a lot about life. He always seemed to have money and could buy whatever he wanted to buy.

They enjoyed being together and measured distance in time and not in miles. According to the formal Mennonite dating process, lovers saw each other only on Sundays. As they got to know each other better, soon Peter and Sara added Wednesday as another date night.

Rain or shine, Sara knew she could count on Peter to be there. When you travel by horse and buggy, bad weather can present an unforeseen problem, but not for Peter; he came prepared. Under the buggy seat, he had a roll of plastic film. Should it begin to rain, to keep neat and dry, he simply wrapped himself in plastic.

Sara Dyck knew they were falling in love. Peter was a rather short guy, but he had big plans and she liked that. Sara came from a home where they only had their basic needs met. There was no money for the nicer things in life. Peter Thiessen always seemed to have more than enough cash in his pocket and Sara liked that too.

Only seventeen, Sara was fairly young, but already marriage was on her mind. There were other girls in the village who had married at that age and she thought she was ready. While she was young in years, there was a maturity about her that not every other girl had. She liked the idea of having her own home, and doing things her own way.

Sara and Peter had talked seriously about marriage, but they faced a big problem. In their Mennonite tradition, you did not get married until after you had joined the Church. Sara accepted this as a way of life. It was the passage into adulthood and she was willing to do it. For Peter it was a different story.

For reasons of his own, Peter did not want to make the "Church commitment." Peter's father had put business ahead of spiritual things and he was following in his father's footsteps. Also, in his heart, Peter wanted to be honest. There were just too many church rules and regulations. He knew he could never keep them all.

Like most other Mennonite families in Mexico, Sara's family had very little open discussion about spiritual things. Faith was considered a private matter of the heart. However, before and after each meal, it was customary to pray a short prayer of blessing on the food and to offer a prayer of thanksgiving after the meal.

Until they were out of school, children were not actively involved in the local Old Colony Mennonite Church. However, in their late teens or early twenties, church membership was an assumed prerequisite before anyone could be married with the blessing of the Church.

Sara had discussed baptism with her parents and they thought she was old enough to take this important step of faith. Joining the Church was her own personal decision. This is how she had been raised and to her it was the right thing to do. Sara had made up her mind; "Yes, she wanted to become a member in the Old Colony Mennonite Church."

More than just studying the Church Catechism, it was also a time of introspection. The church leaders challenged the baptismal candidates to examine their personal lives. Were they living a clean moral life? Had they confessed their sins to God? Were they doing things in their private life that were not in keeping with the rules of the church?

The Old Colony Mennonite Church certainly recognized and honored Jesus coming as the Savior of the world. But the message of God's grace seemed limited to the forgiveness of our sins. After the confession and forgiveness of sins, it was then up to each person to live a Godly life in their own strength. Who was able to do that?

Joining the Church was a six week process. Each of the young people involved had to attend all of the required church services. During this time there was a focus on the questions and answers in the Catechism. Each applicant was expected to know the answers and be able to recite them verbatim.

The doctrinal teachings in the Catechism were true to the scriptures. It began with the knowledge of God as our creator and included the virgin birth of Jesus and his death on the cross, followed by the resurrection. The Catechism presented the basic message of the Gospel in a simple and understandable way.

After the Catechism classes were completed, each baptismal candidate had a "one on one" meeting with the church elders. This was a serious event and the church leaders wanted to make sure the young people were aware of the big step they were taking. If there was something in their lives they needed to confess, this was the time to do it.

Baptism was more than joining the Church. It was a public declaration of faith in Jesus as Savior. This was an important doctrine that distinguished Menno Simons from Martin Luther. It is still a major distinction between Mennonites and Lutherans as well as Catholics.

Both Catholics and Lutherans practice infant baptism. Menno Simons was convinced that baptism was only to be administered to those who were adults and had made a profession of personal faith in Jesus Christ. This was also the doctrinal position of the Old Colony Mennonite Church.

Finally the day of the Baptism arrived. Dressed in black, the baptismal candidates knelt before the bishop. Each one was asked to verbally affirm his or her faith in Jesus Christ as Lord and Savior. Pouring the baptismal water on each person's head, the bishop then pronounced, "I baptize you in the name of the Father, the Son and the Holy Spirit."

The bishop then would take each candidate by the hand. As they rose from their kneeling position, he would recognize them as brothers and sisters in the Lord. This was followed by an official welcome as a new member in the Old Colony Mennonite Church.

Baptism was followed by the first communion for each of the young people. To the members joining the Old Colony Mennonite Church, this was a happy event. They were now members in good standing in the Church. If it was on their agenda, they were also ready to get married.

It was a great day for Sara Dyck. She knew she had made the right decision. This had been the most serious time in her life spiritually. More than just praying during meals or at bed time, Sara had also started praying during the day. Not loud or long prayers, just whispers to God, asking for his help. But she was also praying for Peter.

Sara and Peter were serious in their relationship and marriage was on their minds. But how could they get married, if Peter did not join the Church? Leave it to Peter; he had a plan. Sara's parents had taken a liking to Peter. They enjoyed having him in the house. But there was also a bit of suspicion. Peter moved fast and always seemed to be a step ahead of everybody else. What would he be doing next?

Sara knew Peter's plan. They had talked about it, and she was willing to go with him, wherever it might lead. Peter would go to Canada and while he was there, he would become a member in the Old Colony Church. In Canada the Church did not have so many "do's and don'ts," and owning a car was not a problem. The dress code was also much more relaxed.

Sara's parents had no problem with Peter visiting Canada. What they did not know; Peter was planning to come back and take their daughter Sara with him to Canada. Soon they were going to find out.

O CANADA
The True North Strong and Free

Peter Thiessen had heard much about Canada. He had also met lots of Canadians but he had never actually been to Canada. This was his first trip and as they approached the Canadian Customs, he was a little nervous. He knew that clearing customs should be relatively easy, but Peter had a question he wanted to ask the officer in charge.

Since his father had been born in Canada, getting a Canadian passport had been easy for him. Talking to the Canadian Customs officer, he explained his situation. He wanted to bring his girl friend Sara Dyck, to Canada. They wanted to get married, but she did not have a Canadian passport to Canada.

As Peter explained their plans to the Customs official, the officer gave him a simple answer; "Get legally married in Mexico, and then bring her to Canada as your wife." That seemed simple enough to Peter, but how could he ever explain it to Sara and her family? In the Mennonite tradition, you only get married in the church. This was something that he would have to think about.

After clearing Canada Customs at Emerson, Manitoba, it was just a few more miles and they would arrive in the town of Winker. They were just a short distance from the village where Peter's grandparents had lived some fifty years ago.

Coming from Mexico to Canada had been a long trip and they were glad it was over. As Peter and his traveling partners drove into the thriving town he felt at home. Most of the people he met in Winkler also had Mennonite family names that he recognized.

Many of them no doubt, were distant family relatives. Although everyone in Canada had attended public school and spoke English, still most of the folks living in the Winkler area also spoke Low German. To Peter it was almost like being back in Mexico.

This was January, in the middle of the Canadian winter. What really got to Peter is how cold it was outside. Cold weather in Mexico meant the temperature might go below the freezing level. Here in Canada, if you were not careful and dressed properly, you might freeze to death!

Another thing Peter noticed, it seemed that every car had an electrical cord coming out from under the hood. He knew that car batteries have to be charged. Maybe they should get new batteries, he thought to himself.

He soon discovered that the power cords were connected to an engine block heater designed to keep the engine warm. Without being plugged in overnight, likely the cars would not start on a cold Manitoba winter morning.

Now it was time to unpack and find a place to live. Peter knew he had close relatives living in the Winkler area. He had brought the names of several of his uncles and aunts, and had their phone numbers. He was sure they would want to hear about the Thiessen families living in Mexico. At the same time, it could provide a temporary place for him to stay, while he looked for a job.

Peter was right. When he called his extended family members in Winkler, they were excited. "Yes! come on over," they beamed. By the time he arrived, there was food on the table. While they were eating the questions began, "Did you bring any pictures? Are your parents still alive and well? Are you married? Are you planning to get married?" The questions went on and on.

What Peter needed to know was, "Could he stay at their house, maybe for just thirty days?" He knew it would not take him very long to get settled down and find a job. He wanted to have his own place to live. Peter wasn't asking for charity; that had never been his style. He was willing to pay rent, even for the first month.

Sure enough, his relatives were generous and made him feel welcome in their home. They were going to provide room and board to him at a low monthly price. They were enjoying Peter. His outgoing personality made it fun to have him in the house. Peter had lots of stories to tell. He was great entertainment.

Almost immediately, Peter started looking for a job. He kept his plans to himself, but he had a tight schedule. He needed to find work, get a place to live, join the Church, save some money and then go back to Mexico where Sara was waiting for him to come and get her. Together they would start a new life in Canada.

Peter had good mechanical skills and was also an exceptionally good welder. Winkler had several manufacturing plants and he was confident that he could find a good job quickly. Peter soon discovered that coming from Mexico to Manitoba had a liability. There were some other Mennonite families who had returned to Canada from Mexico, who had not behaved well.

Some of them had been lazy and were unreliable in the work place. Still others were drunks and not trustworthy. Peter knew he could overcome all that. He had confidence in himself; he was a good worker and also a good salesman. He would simply sell himself to the employer.

Knowing he would only be there for a short time, Peter was not fussy about what he did, but he did want a good paying job. He needed to start saving money immediately. He was ready to give his best to whoever was going to hire him, but he also wanted a good paycheck in return.

Soon he found the job he wanted. He would be a welder in a fabrication plant. Not only did it offer good pay, it also allowed him to work extra hours and that meant overtime pay. Peter enjoyed what he was doing, but his mind was also on Sara. He missed her and was making plans to go back to Mexico and get her. But first he had to join the Church.

There was an Old Colony Mennonite Church in the village of Chortitz, four miles south of the town of Winkler where Peter now lived and worked. He decided to visit the church one Sunday morning. He discovered that the church services were a lot like they were in Mexico, except here everybody came to church by car and Peter liked that.

After the church service he waited to meet the bishop. Peter introduced himself as coming from Mexico but now living in Winkler. To the delight of the bishop, Peter told him that he would like to join the Church.

He then asked the bishop if he would officiate at their wedding, after he and Sara would come back to Canada. The bishop knew Peter had more than Church membership on his mind, but that was fine. After all, wedding and funerals were part of the mission of the church.

Many of those attending the church that morning had uncles, aunts and cousins still living in Mexico. They were happy to meet Peter. He was someone who knew their distant relatives and could give them a family update.

Peter had made the decision, and now it was time to begin the Church membership program. The classes were a part of the regular Sunday morning service. The bishop and all the other church leaders had all been to Canadian schools and spoke English, still all the Old Colony Church services were conducted in the German language.

This made it easier for Peter with the required Catechism classes. What little schooling he had in Mexico had also been in German. Peter was pleased to discover that the Church Catechism they were studying was the same one they had used at the Church school in Mexico. He had always had a good memory and could still recall many of the answers to the Catechism questions.

Although he felt that what he was doing was good and proper, honestly Peter was more interested in getting church membership behind him. His overriding goal was to be able to get married to Sara Dyck and to do so with the blessing of their families as well as the Church.

Finally the day of his baptism arrived. There were only about four other young men and women joining the Church at that time. As they knelt on the floor before the bishop, Peter recognized that this was a solemn moment. He was making a profession of faith in Jesus Christ, as well as a promise to God that he wanted to live the way a Christian should live.

There were no telephones in the Mennonite homes in Mexico, but there were businesses close by that did have phones. Peter knew who to call to get a message to Sara. He wanted her to know that he had been baptized and joined the Old Colony Mennonite Church in Chortitz, Manitoba.

Sara also needed to know that he would be on his way to get her shortly. And yes, as he already had told her, the plan still was that they were going to get legally married in Cuauhtémoc, Mexico. Then when they got back to Canada, they would really get married in the church.

He had only been in Canada four months, but already Peter had bought a nice car. It was a 1965 Pontiac Bonneville, with a powerful V8 engine. He was sure that he could make the trip to

Mexico and come back to Canada without having any major mechanical car problems.

In just a few days, Peter was on his way back to Mexico. It was a long drive of well over 2,000 miles. He maybe didn't know it, but he would make this trip many times in the days that lay ahead. For the moment he had only one thing on his mind. He and Sara would get married in Mexico and then return to Canada.

Peter and his traveling partners had been on the road for two days. That is when Peter smelled something. The car seemed to be running hot. He looked at the engine gauges, and sure enough, the car engine was overheating. This could be big trouble. Having the car repaired at a Pontiac dealership could be very expensive.

Here is what they would do; they would fix the car engine themselves. Soon they were parked in a vacant lot. They had lots of mechanic's tools in the trunk and knew how to use them, Peter was sure that they would have to pull the heads on the V8 engine, and it would not be an easy task, but they had no option.

Two days of hard work and the engine was re-assembled. They were ready to hit the road again. As the miles flew by, they knew they were getting close to Texas, one of the states that border Mexico. Then it happened. There was that hot smell again. Yes, the heat gauge was showing hot again as they glided to a stop on the parking lot of the service station.

Again they repeated the entire process; pull the heads, buy more gaskets, oil and engine coolant etc. But Peter knew there had to be something that was causing the problem.

He spoke to a mechanic at an engine shop who said, "You have to machine the heads." Peter knew what that meant and being mechanically inclined, it made sense to him. Following the advice of the mechanic, he made the repairs properly.

Peter had spent most of his available cash and they still had a good distance to drive. If this repair would not last, they could be in deep trouble. The next morning as they fired up the engine, it was running smoothly. Again they were ready to hit the road. In his heart Peter was praying, "Lord help us to get to Mexico, before the engine quits again."

They were pleased; the repair had worked and the engine temperature was staying normal. The last miles of the trip seemed to drag on. Peter had been gone for five months. It had been too long to be away from the girl he loved. When he spotted her house, his heart began to race. Then he saw her, standing there, more beautiful than ever. As he parked the car, he couldn't wait to hold her in his arms.

Arriving in Mexico with his flashy Pontiac, he was scorned by some and admired by others. Word was out that Peter had joined the Church in Canada and the local church leaders were not happy. In their minds he was being sneaky. He wanted the blessing and covering of the church but still live, what they considered to be a worldly life style.

Knowing the problem they had with his car, Peter was about ready to trade it for a horse and buggy. At least horses did not blow head gaskets or overheat. But then, he was only playing a game in his mind. He believed the last engine repair would take him and Sara, back to Canada without any more trouble.

Now there was no time to lose. They needed to go to Cuauhtémoc and have the judge perform the legal wedding. With a Catholic background, the Mexican people held marriage in high esteem. Because Sara was just seventeen years of age, she was considered to be under legal age. She needed the written consent of her father.

Both Peter's and Sara's father joined them at the courthouse where the judge was waiting to sign the wedding papers. There was no music and no wedding march. Just two young people making a promise that they would be true to each other as they became husband and wife.

With a smile, in the romantic Spanish language, the presiding judge said, "I now pronounce you man and wife. What God has joined together, let not man separate."

There was no fanfare or celebration after the ceremony. As far as Peter and Sara were concerned, this was a legal family affair. They would not be considered legitimately married until it was done at the church in Canada. Still Peter knew that Sara was his. She would be his for the rest of his life.

The days that followed were bitter sweet. In just a few more days they would be leaving for Canada. Sara was excited about the new life that lay ahead. Peter had shared about the good living conditions she would have when they got back and she liked that. But the thought of saying "Good bye" to her mother and father and her eleven brothers and sisters was painful. Would she ever see them again?

Having lived in Mexico for over twenty years, Peter had lots of friends. He enjoyed telling them what living in Canada was all about. After all, he was almost a world traveler. Not many other young men his age had even been outside of the borders of Mexico, much less gone to Canada.

The last day came too quickly. It was something that Sara had avoided thinking about. The car was loaded with her most important personal belongings. Like most other Mennonite women, Sara's mother was a good cook. She had packed food and homemade treats for Sara and Peter to enjoy on their long journey north to Canada.

Through tears and hugs, Sara and Peter said their farewells, first to Sara's family and then to Peter's mother and father. Now it was time to go. Leaving the Mennonite village where they had both grown up was not easy. There were so many memories of good times they had enjoyed and the hard times were easy to forget.

Peter Thiessen and Sara returned from Mexico to Canada, and like the customs official had promised, going through Canada customs with Sara was smooth sailing. All they had to do was show the legal documents that they were husband and wife, legally married in Mexico.

The sun was setting as Peter and Sara pulled into Winkler, Manitoba, the town they would now call their home. Peter already had some friends and acquaintances, but it was all new to Sara except for some family relatives.

Soon the word was out that Peter and Sara were planning to get married. Sara needed a place to live until the wedding. She was invited to live with her uncle and aunt. They were family members Sara had never met before.

TRIPLE E TRAILERS was one of the bigger employers in Winkler, Manitoba. The company had been started by a local businessman, Peter W. Enns. It was fast becoming a leading manufacturer in the travel trailer and motor homes industry in Canada. **LOADMASTER,** another Winkler manufacturing company, was a sub-contractor to **TRIPLE E TRAILERS.**

Here is where Peter had a job waiting. He was making 90¢ per hour. This was 1970 and that was the going rate for that type of work. Peter had an idea. He went to the boss and asked him for a raise. "If I work twice as hard as the other employees, will you increase my pay," he asked?

Skeptical about the proposal, but impressed by Peter's audacity, Mr. Loewen, the owner of the company said, "Yes." Putting his ingenuity to work, it wasn't long before Peter had doubled his pay. He was making $1.80 per hour and receiving a $5 per project bonus, for the work he was doing.

Peter Thiessen and Sara were going to get married. Now they needed a house. Not just any house; he wanted a nice home for Sara. She was going to be his queen and he wanted her to have the best. Mr. Loewen, the President of **LOADMASTER,** liked Peter and the way that he worked. He even agreed to be a co-signer to the note, and helped them with the purchase of their first house.

Now it was time to make plans for the "Real wedding." Peter had already joined the Old Colony Mennonite Church in the village of Chortitz, just four miles south of Winkler. The Church in Canada had fewer rules than the Church in Mexico. Peter thought that maybe he could keep them. He was willing to give it a try.

August 9, 1970 was the day of Peter and Sara's wedding. It was a simple Sunday afternoon event. Old Colony Mennonite weddings always were simple. Only a few outside guests had come to witness the occasion.

Sara wore a black dress, and Peter a white shirt but without a necktie. (Neckties were considered too worldly) The wedding reception was typical. It was limited to buns and bologna, sugar cubes and coffee.

After an overnight honeymoon, it was back to work for Peter. He had already bought their first house and it was beyond Sara's wildest dreams.

This was their first opportunity to have a house of their own and Sara loved it. Born and raised in Mexico, in a house without electricity or any plumbing conveniences, this was a little bit of heaven on earth.

Homesick for Family
Sara wants to go Home

Leaving Mexico and moving north to Manitoba, Canada, had been good for Peter & Sara Thiessen. It was an educational experience for both of them. With his limited formal schooling, Peter was learning many valuable lessons in business and in the school of hard knocks.

He also discovered the importance of speaking the English language. Although he was not fluent and had a very limited vocabulary, Peter had no problem communicating his message. In the years to come it would become a valuable asset to him in building a world class business.

Peter never seemed to be out of work. If he couldn't find a job, he could always buy and sell something. In addition to his selling skills, like most of the young men who grew up on the farm in Mexico, Peter had mechanical abilities that served him well. He was a good welder. Winkler had many different manufacturing enterprises that provided great employment opportunities, especially to those with welding skills. As the heartland of the Mennonite community in Southern Manitoba, Winkler was a good place to work, as well as to raise a family.

Peter and Sara Thiessen were newlyweds. Just like in every marriage there were adjustments that had to be made. One of their advantages was the fact that families on both sides were many miles away. There were no e-mails and even telephone service to Mexico was only used for emergency purposes.

Consequently there was little interference from either side of the family. That also meant Sara had no one else to talk to about problems she might have or decisions she needed to make. Of course as husband and wife, the best advice is to be rational and make decisions on facts.

In any marriage relationship, there can be times when there is a lack of communication, as well as times when there is too much spoken. Not talking enough easily leads to misunderstanding and quick harsh words spoken in anger can cause wounds that take a long time to heal.

Those are the times when the ear of a father or mother, or brother and sister are missed the most. Peter and Sara had those moments. In many ways they were opposites. Perhaps that's why they had fallen in love in the first place. We've all heard the saying, "Opposites attract."

This was certainly true in their marriage. He made decisions quickly; she wanted to think about it. Peter needed lots of friends; Sara needed only a few friends. Living in Winkler, she felt like she was among strangers without any really close friendships.

There were distant cousins and other relatives they saw from time to time, but still she felt alone. The Church where they now both were members had mostly older ladies. True to the name, they were very old fashioned and Sara just did not seem to fit into their life style.

Sara appreciated the wonderful home she and Peter had been able to buy. It really was too big for just two people, but then it wasn't long before Sara discovered that she was pregnant and was excited about having their first baby.

Both Sara and Peter had been born in Mexico; now their baby was going to be born in Canada. That would make them an international family. Peter kind of liked the idea, never dreaming that at some point they would also get to call the United States of America their home.

It was a normal pregnancy for Sara and after nine months they had a healthy little baby boy. In keeping with the family tradition, he was named Peter, a very common Mennonite name, he was named after his father, Peter Thiessen.

Now there would be three generations in the family, with that name; Peter Thiessen, the grandfather who had migrated to Mexico in the 1920s, Peter, the husband of Sara, and the new arrival, Peter Jr. They were doing their part to carry on the family name.

Taking care of her new baby, Sara began to miss her family even more. She wanted their son to grow up knowing his grandparents and they were many miles away. She sent pictures of their new home and the baby and on a rare occasion, talked with her Mother and Father by phone. However, just hearing their voices made her more homesick.

Sara would never forget the morning she got that dreadful phone call from Mexico. "Sara, your Dad has passed away!" That was all she needed to hear; her mind went into fast forward. This would mean an immediate trip back to Mexico. When Peter heard the sad news, he needed no persuasion. Family was important and he was ready to go.

Within twenty four hours they were on the road going back to be with Sara's family at this most difficult time. Stopping only for gas and hamburgers at fast food restaurants, Peter drove on into the night. By now Peter had made this trip on several different occasions, but this time they had set a record.

They had made it back to Mexico in just thirty-six hours. Peter and Sara and their new baby were greeted with hugs and kisses but also with tears. Sara's father had passed away unexpectedly. After suffering a major heart attack he had died almost instantly. While it was good to see her family again, still Sara was sad.

She knew she would miss her father and the fact that her father would never see his little grandson Peter; at least not on this earth, added to her sorrow. The next couple of days seemed like a blur. It was bittersweet. The day of the funeral was a sad event.

A husband, father and grandfather had suddenly been taken away. Saying good-bye to someone you love is never easy. In this case Sara knew she would not see her father again in her life time. Still, she believed that one day in the resurrection, they would meet again.

Then there were good moments. Her friends wanted to know about her new house and how she liked living in Canada; something Sara really did not want to talk about. But soon it was going to be time to say one more good-bye. Sara knew they needed to go back to Canada again.

Peter had a job waiting and life had to go on. Few words were spoken as they headed back through Texas on the long road back to Winkler Manitoba. Little Peter was walking, but still in diapers when Sara discovered she was pregnant again.

It was normal for an expectant mother to have mood swings, but Peter could tell Sara was not happy. It wasn't another pregnancy that got her upset. It was being alone in a strange country, away from her family, and now especially her mother and her sisters.

After the passing of her father, from time to time Sara would talk to Peter about possibly moving back to Mexico. It was something Peter could not understand. In Canada they had everything a young family could wish for. He had a good job and they had a beautiful house, a car and fancy appliances. What more could anyone ask for?

While they were dating and the first months in their marriage, they were madly in love. But now Sara began to recognize things in Peter that she did not like. He was too impulsive. He had a short temper. He made decisions without asking for her opinion.

Sometimes when he spoke harshly she would feel hurt, although she tried not to show it. Sara had little to say in the choice of their friends. For the most part they were Peter's friends, and she just came along for the ride.

What made it even more difficult was that most of Peter's acquaintances, like Peter, enjoyed taking a drink. Sara knew that drinking can create many other problems. She had seen it in other families and she wanted no part of it.

When her second pregnancy came to full term, Sara and Peter had another beautiful baby. This time it was a little girl. Peter and Sara named her Lisa. Peter thought they had the perfect family. He had a good wife; they had two sweet children, money in the bank, a good house and a thriving business.

Sara had been waiting for the right moment. "Peter," she began, "I have been thinking that maybe we should move back to Mexico." "She can't be serious," Peter thought to himself. Who would want to give up a good house and all the modern things they had, and go back to the hard life they had known before coming to Canada?

It wasn't that Sara didn't appreciate what Peter had so generously provided for her. But if she had to choose between things and relationships with other people, and especially her family; the family wins. Much later in life, Sara was going to learn that you can have both; a great home, lots of good things, as well as good family relationships.

Peter had been working at **LOADMASTER** for over three years now. He had seen good increases in pay and their bank account was growing. This was all very important to him. But then he also wanted to see Sara happy. They had argued some and there had been hard words, but down deep he loved her and he knew she loved him too.

Peter enjoyed the work he was doing, but he would enjoy it even more if he was the boss. The idea of eventually having his own business seemed appealing to him. In Mexico he had learned how to work hard; in Canada he was learning how to work smart.

Maybe it was time to go back to Mexico and start a new business. Normally Peter spoke his mind quickly, but now he was taking his time. He did not want to promise Sara something that he could not give her. Then the day came when he was ready.

When Peter told Sara about what he had been thinking she was beside herself. It was useless for her to try and hide her feelings. "Was this really going to happen?" she wondered to herself.

Sometimes Sara had accused Peter of not listening to what she had to say. Now she was sorry. He had been listening; he just needed time to think about it. At least that is how she was seeing things at the moment.

Peter and Sara had lived in Canada almost three years when they decided they would move back to Mexico. Peter was confident that like his father he too could be successful in buying farm equipment. There was lots of good equipment available in the United States and farmers in Mexico were doing well. This was the right time to go into business.

Over the past years, the house they had purchased had appreciated substantially in value. If they sold it there would be a good profit. That, plus what they had in savings would be more than $25,000. He knew he had enough capital to get started in the used farm equipment business.

Peter had always liked fancy cars. It would be nice to drive back to Mexico in a sporty car. Peter had his eye on a late model black Plymouth Barracuda. It was a sporty two door car with a V8 engine. He was sure it would catch everybody's attention in the village where they had been raised. Peter liked the idea and made the purchase.

Now it was time to put the house up for sale. The housing market in Winkler was strong and they should be able to get a good price. It was just like he had imagined; the house sold quickly, at a good price and a good profit. They were almost ready to make the move.

In the years they spent in Winkler, they had accumulated a lot of stuff. Kitchen appliances, furniture, yard tools, everything had to go; price didn't really matter, they took whatever they could get. Always generous at heart, Peter ended up giving away about as much as he sold.

It was almost like 1922, when their grandparents had made the first move to Mexico. The difference was that Peter and Sara knew where they were going and what to expect when they got there. They also would have family waiting for them when they arrived.

For Sara, saying "Good Bye" to Winkler was easy. All she could think of was seeing her family again. Then too, she had the confidence that Peter would provide a good home for them when they got back to Mexico.

The car was loaded, the tank was full of gas and they had cash in their pocket. Peter and Sara were both excited as they crossed the US border on their way home.

Empresario

An Entrepreneur in Any Language

Seeing her family again was on Sara's mind, as they headed south on Interstate 29 going toward Kansas City, Missouri. To Peter Thiessen it was all business. He was an *empresario*!

In the early 1800s before Texas was a State, Spain was in control of Mexico. For a short period of time, the country of Spain granted residents of Texas the right to settle on Mexican land. In exchange the Texans were to recruite new settlers. Those brave Texans were called *empresarios*, the Spanish word for "entrepreneurs."

Peter was of German descent and in the German lnaguage, "unternehmer" has a similar meaning. A direct translation could be "undertaker." Not the funeral home kind, rather it describes someone who is willing and able to undertake the implementation and completion of an idea.

"*Empresario, unternehmer, entrepreneur*," in any language, Peter Thiessen was the embodiment of the word. Obviously not something he had learned in school, it was a gift; a part of his DNA. Today Peter would say: "It's a gift from God." While others may be called to teach, preach, practice medicine, design equipment or even write a book, he knew that he was called to be a businessman.

Business may have been in his blood, but still the gift would require development. Some of what he needed to know could have come from school learning. However the most valuable lessons would come from the "school of hard knocks." Here the test was trial and error. Sometimes not passing the test, meant doing it over again and Peter had some of those experiences as well.

As they were heading south, each time they passed a used farm equipment dealer, Peter wondered if there was anything on the lot he could buy and resell. One of the most reliable and well-known brands was John Deere. From the small John Deere B tractors, to gigantic harvest combines, there was a need for them down in Mexico and he wanted to be in the middle of each transaction.

Miles passed quickly and soon they were in the state of Oklahoma and heading for Texas. Peter knew many of the smaller cities and towns. He had been there before with his father. This is where his father had purchased most of the tractors and other related farm machinery that he later resold to the Mennonite farmers in Mexico.

He had cash in his pocket; about twenty thousand dollars. Why wait until they arrived in Mexico? He could start buying equipment immediately. Always quick to make decisions, Peter told Sara what he was thinking. She wanted to get to see her family as soon as possible, but reluctantly she agreed. She knew once Peter had something in his mind, he usually didn't change it, so why try.

By the time they got to the Mexican border, Peter had stopped at a countless number of farm equipment dealers. He had purchased more than a dozen pieces of equipment. With the inventory he now had, Peter could see himself in the used equipment business. All he needed was to hire a truck to bring the equipment into Mexico.

The day they arrived back home, in the Mennonite village, north of Cuauhtémoc, was a big event. The word had spread quickly that Peter and Sara Thiessen were returning from Canada. Sara's mother and her family were anxious to see the new grandchildren and Sara couldn't wait to show them off.

Although Sara had not really enjoyed living in Canada, there were some things that she had picked up. This was particularly true in the area of dress. She liked the way some of the modern dresses looked and the way they fit. She knew that Peter liked them too. She tried not to be conspicuous, but still it showed that her taste had changed. All the Mennonite women in Mexico dressed ultra conservatively. Sara stood out like a rose in a thorn patch.

Little Peter and Lisa at first were somewhat shy. But it didn't take long before they were on Grandma's lap. The little ones had no idea they had so many relatives. There must have been a hundred or more that tried to hold them and kiss them. Sara knew her family was pleased to have her home again.

Peter's reception was somewhat different. First off, who owned the car he was driving? He was now a member of the Church, and surely he knew that owning an automobile was strictly forbidden. On the other hand, there were other young men who envied Peter. They admired what he was doing, but did not have the nerve to follow his example.

Peter had farm equipment coming in from Texas, and needed a place to unload and display his inventory. Property ownership was important to him. He wanted to have his own place. Not just any place, he wanted lots of room. He always had growth in mind. In everything he did, Peter always planned to do things in a big way. Here was his problem; although he had joined the Church in Canada, he still was not in good standing with the local Church leadership in Mexico. He knew that the purchase of any property in the area was under the control of the Church.

Driving his Barracuda up and down the village roads only added fuel to the fire. But leave it to Peter; he had an idea. He would take in a new business partner who was a member "in good standing" with the Church.

Then they could purchase the needed property and start the farm equipment business. They would simply put the title to the land in the name of his new business partner.

Having a partner also meant that there would be someone on the lot to sell the used farm equipment while Peter was out on a buying trip in the United States. The idea worked without a hitch. He had a brother-in-law Jake Krahn, who had the needed qualifications. When Peter offered him the partnership proposal, he readily accepted it.

There was a piece of land adjacent to the highway that Peter had his eyes on. It had good frontage with plenty of room toward the back of the property for future expansion. This was an ideal spot for a used farm equipment lot. Ultimately this was also where Peter would build a house for his family, and in the days to come, establish several other businesses.

In just a few days they were in possession of the land and the used farm equipment business was in operation. Truckloads of used machinery began arriving almost every week. Soon it was the talk of the villages. "Peter Thiessen was back from Canada and he was bringing a new supply of used farm equipment." There was no shortage of customers and business was booming.

For the moment Peter and Sara and the children were staying with Sara's mother. But with two small children, they really needed a home of their own. Not just any home, Peter wanted a good house for Sara and their family. He had liked all the modern conveniences they had in Canada and he wanted Sara to enjoy the same standard of living in Mexico.

Rather than buying a house, Peter decided they would build a new home on the property they had just purchased. Peter was more of a mechanic than he was a carpenter. He wanted the house to be built right, so he hired a good builder for the new home construction project.

The Church leadership had been watching the activity of the business. They were aware that Peter was the driving force in the partnership, but since he was not a member of the Church, they zeroed in on his partner. After being in business just six months, Jake Krahn, his brother-in-law as well as his business partner, came to talk to Peter.

The elders had been talking to Jake about his being a business partner with Peter Thiessen. They had let him know, they did not approve. "Peter," Jake began, "it is a sin for you to own a car." He continued, "It is also a sin for us to be making so much money." Peter knew about the car ownership rules, but how could making a profit be a sin? That was the main reason he had gone into business.

Peter knew Jake was serious. To keep peace in the family something would have to be done, and soon. "I'll sell the car," Peter announced. "And I am going to buy a horse and buggy." It was hard for his brother-in-law to believe what Peter was saying. He wondered, "Would Peter actually do it?" That was also the question on Sara's mind. She knew Peter liked cars. Was he really going to drive a horse and buggy? Soon time would tell.

The Plymouth Barracuda Peter owned was a beautiful black car with a V8 engine. He knew it would sell quickly, especially at the right price. Peter was willing to offer the car for sale at a sacrifice price to satisfy his business partner and to keep the church leadership off his back.

The Barracuda had not yet been imported into Mexico, so Peter drove it to El Paso, Texas to make the sale. Asking just $1,800, the car sold quickly. As he watched the car drive away, for a moment he wondered, "Did I do the right thing?"

Peter had asked a friend to follow him and give him a ride back to the village in Mexico. Now Peter had no transportation, but then he had promised he would buy a horse and buggy. True to his word, he began looking to see what he could find.

There were no "horse and buggy" dealers in the village, so it would have to be a private sale. Not just any horse and buggy would do. Peter wanted the deluxe version. He needed a horse that looked good and was fast as well as a first class buggy to match.

When he finally found what he liked, the owner was asking $1,900! That was more than he had gotten for his Barracuda. Without dickering or wasting time, Peter bought the rig. He had gone from a car with a V8 engine and one hundred and eighty-five horsepower, to a buggy with just one horse power and added $100 cash to make the deal.

The horse's name was Queen. She was a show piece and horse lovers admired his new mode of transportation. For the moment he also had the respect of the men in Church leadership. Peter had done what few others would be willing to do and they admired him for his courage.

Based on Peter's membership in the Church in Canada and in response to his contrition, the elders made the decision to extend the hand of fellowship and recognize Peter as a member in the local church. Sara was pleased but a little suspicious. Peter didn't always tell Sara why he did certain things. She was trying to figure out what really was on his mind. Soon she would find out.

Three months down the road, Peter realized that a horse and buggy simply could not meet his transportation needs. The business required him to go the United States several times each month for the purchase of more farm machinery. Hiring someone to drive him was not practical; he was willing to face the consequences, whatever they might be.

Seeking only the approval of his wife Sara, Peter decided to buy a new truck. He went into town to see the local Chevrolet dealer. He found just what he needed; a brand new Chevy pickup truck. As he drove back into the village with his new purchase, the Church leadership was in an uproar.

After Peter had sold his Barracuda they had accepted him into the Church as a member in good standing. He had confessed the sin of owning an automobile and also promised not to do it again. This was no small thing; now he had deliberately broken the Church rules. They had no option; Peter had to be excommunicated.

Thursday was always the day when the Church leaders met to discuss disciplinary action against any of the membership. Peter Thiessen's name was the first one on the list. He was a bad influence on other young men and they would not put up with his behavior. Unanimously they voted for his expulsion. Peter would be excommunicated from the Church.

Being excommunicated did not seem to matter much to Peter, but it did affect Sara. Her family members were all in good standing in the Church. Sara knew that she could go with them to attend the weekly service. But she wanted her husband to be with her, and she knew he was not welcome.

Having lived in Canada for three years, she wondered, "Was the Church placing too much emphasis on what it considered to be worldliness?" If it was not a sin to own a car in Canada, why was it a sin to own a vehicle in Mexico? Sara wondered about this, but she had no one to ask.

As the days went by, Peter realized that his partner Jake Krahn was not happy. The burden of guilt the Church was putting on him for his association with Peter was too much. To keep peace in the family and satisfy the demands of the Church, Peter agreed to buyout his partner.

Peter may not have been a good example to other young men spiritually, but when it came to business ideas, they were drawn to him. He could make things happen quickly and had a feel about what might or might not work. To him it was common sense, but it truly was an insight that came with his calling as an entrepreneur.

Peter was a busy man, but he was always willing to listen to someone with a good idea. One day Peter Hildebrand, who was also his cousin, came up with a proposal. He wanted to start an oven manufacturing business. There were other ovens on the market, but they were too big for the small houses many of the local Mexicans had.

There seemed to be a need for smaller ovens and it looked like a good idea to Peter. There was a vacant building on his farm equipment property where the ovens could be manufactured. It was time for another partnership to begin. Soon Peter and his cousin Peter Hildebrand were in the oven business. While their main customers were Mexicans, they also included the Mennonite communities in the area.

Mennonites are famous for their homemade foods and most every Mennonite housewife is a good cook. Of course with the typical large families Mennonites have, they get lots of practice and experience. One of the key ingredients in good cooking is having a good cook stove.

When they first settled in the 1920s, cook stoves were part of the inventory they brought from Canada. The stoves they brought were long lasting, but this was fifty years later. It was time to replace the old stoves with new ones. The familiar old saying, "Find a need and fill it," also applied to ovens and cook stoves in Mexico.

The oven and cook stove business began small, but soon it began to grow, and Peter liked that. There was no advertising available nor was it needed. Satisfied customers simply told their friends about the new oven products manufactured by the little company in the Mennonite village.

It wasn't long before retailers in Texas picked up this new brand of smaller ovens. As sales increased, more employees had to be added. Within just two years the business had ten employees and had grown to produce over a thousand ovens per year.

The company had become international in its scope, selling to Mexicans, Mennonites and Americans.

The pioneers, who had come from Canada to Mexico, knew how to improvise. They could make most anything that they needed up to a point. A long time ago, Mennonites had used pegs and wedges to fasten logs and beams, as they built their homes and farm buildings. However, hammers and nails were much easier to use, as well as much faster.

Early on in Canada and then in Mexico, most everything was homemade. Even the tools needed for manufacturing were often made by hand. But these were changing times. Now most of what a household needed or could use was being mass produced.

But even mass produced products had to be marketed and that gave birth to the general store. In more recent times, there were also hardware stores that specialized in items that farmers, housewives and most everyone else could use.

Again, this was another window of opportunity for Peter Thiessen. He had cut his teeth in business as a street vendor selling hardware items. As he thought about it, he realized he had been in the hardware business without even knowing it. He was going to do the same thing; it was simply going to be on a larger scale.

There was room for another business on the farm equipment property. It would be a hardware store. The Mennonites who had settled in Mexico fifty years ago had done well and there was a building boom in the village communities. Sheet metal roofing material was just one of the many items they needed and Peter brought it in by the truckload.

Plumbing supplies, building materials, cement by the bag and whatever else might be needed for construction was available and usually at a good price. A business secret Peter had discovered was to be able to sell at the right price; you first have to be able to buy at the right price and usually that meant buying in volume.

Like most every other venture Peter was involved in, the hardware store business grew and by the second year, the annual sales exceeded $250,000. Business opportunities excited Peter and making a profit was fulfilling to him, but there was something more important than money on his mind. It was the spiritual condition of his aging father.

Jake Thiessen, Peter's father, never had much involvement in spiritual matters. Weddings and funerals, with few exceptions, were the only time he ever stepped into the church. Like his son Peter, to him church rules and regulations didn't make much sense.

Throughout his adult life, alcohol abuse had been a major problem. In addition, there were issues of immoral behavior that were hidden deep in his heart, which had never been addressed. Peter knew, it; his mother knew it; his father knew it, and most importantly, God knew it.

It was very difficult for him, but Peter made the decision to confront his father about these "secret sins," that really were not a secret. Peter was struggling with his own "drinking problem." Almost daily he was asking God for forgiveness. If anyone needed the grace of God, he knew, it was "Peter."

His concern was that his father had never admitted to having immoral adulterous relationships nor confessed his wrong doings. "Dad," Peter began, "you know and I know there are things you have done that have hurt Mom badly. You may have had reasons why you did it, but that still didn't make them right. You are not well; should you die, I want to see you in heaven some day."

"Tell God you are sorry and ask him to forgive you for the wrong things you have done. God loves you and I know he will forgive you. And then, please Dad, when you and Mother are alone, ask her to forgive you as well." Peter was amazed at his own boldness, but he knew this was a serious matter,

At first his father tried to deny that he had been immoral, but Peter knew this was serious and he would not let up. He was a concerned son who loved his dad. Almost at his wits end, Peter decided that he would stay with his father and pray for him, and if necessary he was willing to pray with him.

Hours passed slowly and by late afternoon Peter wondered how this would all end. But then he felt a peace and an assurance that this was in God's hand. Peter knew he couldn't change his father's heart. That was something only God was able to do.

Then his father cleared his voice. Peter knew he wanted to talk. "What is it Dad?" he asked. "Peter, you are right. I have lived a lie and cheated on your mother. Can God ever forgive me? Do you think Mother will ever forgive me?" Peter was no preacher, but suddenly he knew what to say.

"Dad," he said, "Jesus died on the cross and he paid the price for all of our sins. And that includes all the bad things you have done as well. After three days Jesus rose again. In the last book in the Bible, Jesus said that He has the keys to death and hell. That means He is in charge.

To receive God's forgiveness you have to admit that you are a sinner. You need to confess your sins to God. He will forgive you. Then you need to confess the wrong things you did to Mother as well. I don't know if she even wants to forgive you. That is up to her."

Together Peter and his father prayed. It was not an eloquent prayer, but it was a prayer from the heart. Peter knew that his father was sincere. Jake Thiessen acknowledged that he was a sinner and needed God's forgiveness. No doubt, God heard that prayer and forgave Peter's father for his wrongdoings.

The conversation that followed between Peter's father and mother was private. Peter didn't want to be in on it. But in his heart Peter knew that the grace of God was able to not only forgive sins, but was also able to restore the broken relationship between his father and mother.

This was 1976; Peter's father, Jake Thiessen lived three more years. They were good years that both his father and mother enjoyed together. Then in 1979 his father passed away. At the time Peter was back in Canada and unable to return to Mexico in time for the funeral.

When he received the call that his father had died, Peter knew he had done the right thing by praying with him. He had the assurance that he would see his father again in heaven.

Peter whispered a silent "Thank you" to God for his "Amazing Grace" that saves sinners like Peter Thiessen as well as his father Jake Thiessen.

Always Tell the Truth!

So Why Are You Lying to Mommy?

D addy, why are you lying to Mommy? You tell us to always tell the truth, so why are you lying?" Spoken by his four-year-old daughter Lisa, those words cut Peter like a knife. She was right; Peter had been lying.

Not only did the four years old know it, so did Peter. Most importantly God knew it too. As a little boy, growing up in a Mennonite home, Peter had been taught that he must always tell the truth. He had been teaching it to his own young children as well, but now he himself was caught in a lie by his little daughter.

To Peter Thiessen, his handshake was his signature. Keeping his word was an important business principle he tried to live by. But that was not always the case when it came to his family life. His wife Sara was a good and supportive wife, but there were things that Peter did that she did not approve of and he knew it. One of those things was drinking.

Sara had seen firsthand what drinking had done to her father-in-law Jake Thiessen. Peter shared some of the characteristics of his father. Both were good businessmen and provided well for their families. But when they got drunk, their nature changed. They could become mean and verbally abusive and Sara didn't like it.

Peter was a born leader, with a strong personality. Sara had argued and begged for him to stop drinking without success. She had almost given up, except for one thing; she could still pray for Peter. In her own quiet way she kept asking God to help Peter to see the damage he was doing to himself and his young family, including their marriage relationship.

Just that morning Sara had confronted Peter at his office. She had asked him not to drink again and he had agreed. Peter was going into town and Sara asked him to take their two oldest children, Peter Jr. and Lisa with him. They enjoyed going with him because usually it meant stopping at the store to get an extra treat before coming home.

That day was no different. When Peter had finished the business for the day, as they were heading home, he asked, "Should Daddy get you some potato chips and a soda pop?" "Yes," they answered unanimously. Pulling off the road, he coasted into a liquor store parking lot. He had been there before and knew they had the treats for the kids.

He came out of the store with chips and pop in hand for his children. Then it hit him; "Sara is your boss. She is running your life." She was telling him what he could and could not do. In the Mennonite culture, the man was the head of the house. That meant he was the boss and this was the time to prove it.

Peter headed back into the liquor store and purchased a flask of whiskey. Bottle in hand, Peter and the children began the ride home. As they drove down the dusty road, from time to time Peter would try to distract the children so he could "drink and drive."

He asked them to look at the cattle in the field, the birds in the sky, or whatever else he could find. Each time they looked, he would take a gulp of whiskey. By the time they got home, his eyes were red and showed that he had been drinking again.

When they got home, Peter parked the truck. Before going inside, he carefully hid the whiskey bottle behind the seat. No one else knew it was there and he could come back later and finish what was left in the flask. Locking the door of the truck, with the keys in his pocket, Peter and the two little ones went inside the house.

The moment he entered Sara confronted him. "You have been drinking again," she said. "No I haven't," was Peter's response. "You said you wouldn't and you broke your promise," she continued. "Go and look in the mirror. Your eyes are red and I know you are not telling me the truth."

Peter tried to recover, "A Mexican (meaning a non Mennonite) in town gave it to me." Hands behind her back, their little four year old daughter Lisa spoke up: "Daddy, why are you lying to mommy? You tell us to always tell the truth but now you are lying."

Peter was offended by the rebuke of his little daughter, but she was not finished. "You are not walking to hell, you are running because you are afraid you won't get in," she concluded. At that point she pulled out the flask of whiskey she had been holding behind her back and showed it to her father and mother.

"Where did you get that?" Peter asked her in amazement. "A man gave it to me outside," was her casual response. "What man?" Peter wanted to know. "I don't know, but there was a man outside who gave me the whiskey bottle," was her simple child-like answer.

Peter was speechless. "How could this be happening?" he wondered. Going outside, he checked the truck door and it was locked. He took the key and unlocked the door. Sliding his hand behind the seat, he fumbled for the whiskey flask. It was gone!

He knew where he had hidden the bottle and no one else could have taken it. He had locked the truck and he still had the keys in his hand. Peter tried to figure out what was happening, but he had no answer. Beyond a doubt, Peter knew that God was involved in what was going on here.

He had heard about angels. The Catechism called them spirit beings, created by God. Could God have sent an angel to take the whiskey out of the truck and give it to Lisa? Was Jesus, the man Lisa had seen? Peter would never know for sure. But he knew God was watching.

There was a war going on in Peter's mind, but he was not willing to give up. The demon of alcohol had been in his life now for better than ten years. Peter was not ready to make the decision he knew he would have to make if he wanted to have peace in his home as well as in his heart.

That evening Peter had planned to have a barbeque party with some of their friends. It was normal for Peter to bring whiskey to events like this. Even after what had just happened, tonight would still be no exception. Going to his stash of stored liquor, he took three 40 ounce bottles of whiskey, as they headed out the door.

No doubt, the words of his little girl kept ringing in his ears; "Daddy, why are you lying to Mommy?" He knew how to get them out of his mind. He could always take a drink. One drink led to another, and before the evening was over Peter had shown Sara that he was the boss. Or was the demon of alcohol the real boss in Peter's life?

The next morning, when he awoke, Peter asked Sara how they got home the night before. "I drove home," was Sara's mild response. Peter was embarrassed with his uncontrolled desire for alcohol and for his crude behavior when he was drunk. But beyond embarrassment, there was heaviness in his heart that he had to deal with. It was time to make a serious change in his life.

"Sara," Peter began, "I want to ask you to forgive me for the way I have treated you. I have lied to you and made promises I did not keep. As the tears ran down his face, Sara knew that this time Peter was not playing games with her. With a thankful heart she said, "Yes" to his request.

"Please God," Sara had often prayed, "if you can, help Peter to say no to alcohol. And God, help him to find good new friends that do not drink." Giving Peter to God was the best thing she could have done. God loved Peter and had a wonderful plan for him.

Little did Sara know that God would use her four year old daughter Lisa to answer the prayers she had prayed for her husband, Peter. What Sara did not know, there was a secret "sin" Peter was keeping from her.

Hidden deep in his heart was something he had never told Sara. Peter knew he needed to share it with her, but he was not ready to talk to her about it; at least not yet.

A Time to Buy and Time to Sell
At Fifty Cents on the Dollar

Peter and Sara Thiessen had lived in Mexico for the past five years and life had been good to them. They had built a new home; the finest in any of the surrounding villages.

The house had all the modern conveniences, including two bathrooms. Sara liked this house much better than the old one where she had lived with her parents, from birth through her teenage years, until the day she got married.

The house that had been Sara's home as a child now was almost a hundred years old. Built with sun baked dirt bricks, it was still occupied as a home by a young family living in the nearby village. Just like it had been many years ago there was still a functioning outhouse on the yard.

Peter had been able to establish three businesses and they were all doing well. They owned three vehicles; two trucks and a car.

Financially they were in a place, where if they wanted or needed something, they could afford to buy it.

The oven business Peter had started with his cousin Peter Hildebrand was profitable and growing and the village hardware store was also doing well. But the big money producer was still the used implement business.

Tractors that once cost a few hundred dollars now were worth several thousand. In recent years the Church had relaxed its rules about rubber tires on tractors and other equipment. That was a big help. Now Peter was able to bring in pieces of equipment and sell them without any modification.

Some of the farmers still liked to farm with older pieces of equipment. While farmers in the United States and Canada, as well as in many other parts of the world, were using swathers and combines for harvesting, there were still those in Mexico who wanted to use binders and threshing machines.

Peter found a good supply of binders in Minnesota. Some still in good repair were sitting in machine sheds on the farms of the Swedes and Norwegians who lived in that northern most state. Peter was able to buy these almost obsolete pieces at very reasonable prices. The biggest challenge was hauling these bulky machines two thousand miles.

Once they arrived in Mexico, he could ask whatever he thought the market would bear. He had little or no competition. Peter made numerous trips across the United States, with his truck and trailer. He never knew where he would locate the next piece of machinery and he had to be prepared to purchase it on the spot, load it on the trailer and once again head for Mexico.

Dealer reputation was very important to be successful in the used farm equipment business. There was no written guarantee that went with a used piece of farm equipment. However, if something went very wrong, like an engine failure, or a broken transmission, the buyer still looked to Peter to help with the repair.

Knowing the value of a satisfied customer, he did his best to please his clients, even if it meant taking a loss on a certain item. To minimize the risk, Peter liked to buy used equipment from reputable dealers in the United States. This became more important as he began buying and selling higher priced used farm machinery.

Some of the first used tractors Peter bought were priced well below a thousand dollars. To make a fair profit on the purchase, considering the high cost of transporting the equipment to Mexico, he needed to double his money when he made the sale.

Peter had a favorite farm equipment dealer in Texas. In just one year, he purchased more than a hundred tractors from him. They knew each other well and Peter knew he could trust him. Often the purchase was completed by a telephone call, without Peter ever seeing the tractor.

One of the bigger equipment deals Peter made was when he purchased a tractor for eighteen thousand dollars. He certainly was not going to double his money, but a mere 20% markup would give him a profit of three thousand six hundred dollars.

The past five years in the used equipment business had been a good experience. He liked the profitable deals he had made and had money in the bank. What Peter had not enjoyed was being away from home. He missed Sara and the kids, but being away was part of the package when you import equipment into Mexico.

Not only had Peter's business interests grown, so had his family. When they had returned from Canada, he and Sara had two children. Now after five years, they had two more boys. Four children in a Mennonite family was not considered large, but it also wasn't small.

He couldn't explain it, but there was a restlessness in Peter's heart. Living in the Mennonite village, he felt hemmed in. He wanted the business he had started to continue to grow and expand, but he felt like he was continually bumping his head against the ceiling.

Part of the problem of increasing business was the fact that there were less than a hundred thousand Mennonites living in the total of Mexico. Compare that to Canada with about thirty million, or the United States with over three hundred million. In his mind, Peter began thinking about moving back to Canada one more time.

He remembered that Sara had not enjoyed living in Canada, but that was five years ago. He wondered, with Sara's mother having moved to Winkler, would Sara consider going back up north? In any event, Peter was not ready to talk to Sara about what was on his mind; at least not yet.

Often when he was picking up equipment, Peter was alone in his truck. This gave him lots of time to think and for some reason, he could not get Winkler out of his mind. During the years he had worked there, he had met some of the owners and founders of the large manufacturing companies. They had seemed like ordinary people. In fact they even spoke his Low German language. Maybe one day he would own a huge company like they did.

Often when Peter returned from his buying trips, Sara wanted to talk about what had happened while he was gone. Peter noticed that recently she had been very quiet. Was something bothering her, he wondered. Was she stressed out with their four little kids in the house?

It wasn't the kids; it was the other women who lived in the village. Sara felt that she was being ignored by them. She may not have known it, but some of them were jealous of her. Sara drove her own car and wore more fashionable clothes. She and Peter lived in one of the nicest houses in the village and even got to travel some, outside of Mexico.

Peter could see what was happening. Some of the men in the village, including Church leaders had treated him the same way. The only thing was Peter had a thicker skin. He didn't let that bother him much. But Sara was a woman, and women are more sensitive toward hurt feelings. Still Peter didn't want Sara to be unhappy; but what could he do?

"Sara, sometimes I feel like we don't fit in with the rest of the people who live here," Peter began. "We seem to think differently about many things. They think we are worldly; but I believe that we are growing. I don't want anything or anybody to hold us back. Sara, if that means moving back to Canada, I am willing to do it," Peter concluded.

"Peter, I want to do what you want to do," was Sara's response. "If you want to go back to Canada, I am ready to go with you." Over the next couple of weeks they didn't talk much about moving; still it was on their minds constantly. Each in their own way, both Peter and Sara were also praying about it. Was "the possible move" something God had put into their hearts?

Peter had talked about growth; Sara could see it too. Often it is easier to see growth in someone else, than in yourself. That was also true with Peter and Sara. She remembered the time when their little daughter Lisa had confronted Peter about lying. It had made a big impact on Peter. Shortly after that event, he had decided he would quit drinking.

Then there was the time Peter went to talk to his father about making things right between him and God, as well as with Peter's mother. That had not been easy and normally he would have left that responsibility for the Church leaders. But Peter had grown in his own relationship with God. He knew that he needed to talk to his father before it was too late.

Something else Peter had struggled with in their marriage was the courage to say, "I'm sorry, I was wrong." That doesn't come easy to anyone and especially to a strong willed man. But Peter wanted the slate clean between him and God. He had learned by experience, "If you want forgiveness, you have to confess where you did wrong."

Forgiveness was also a contributing factor in deciding whether or not to move back to Canada. Peter and Sara had both felt the hurts of hard words and disapproving glances from Church leaders.

If they moved, would others think they were running away? Some wounds take time to heal; maybe that's what they needed; time to get away and let God do what only He can do.

Peter never liked indecision. "If you are not going to do it, stop talking about it," was Peter's attitude, and he applied it to himself. If they were going to return to Canada, he had three successful businesses he needed to sell, or liquidate. There was the oven manufacturing, the hardware store and the used farm equipment as well as the property, and finally the house they had built.

In Peter's mind, putting it all together, it should be worth at least a half million dollars. There were not many living in the village that had that much cash available, or could even raise it. Peter wanted cash. He didn't want to carry a note or mortgage. Starting out again in Canada, he would need all the capital he could generate.

He liked to talk; sometimes too much. Never shy about what he was doing or planning to do, Peter had spoken to various potential buyers about buying all the assets he had in Mexico. Talk is cheap, and for the most part, he did not take his "prospects" seriously. However there was one man who could possibly be a buyer, Peter thought to himself.

He was waiting for the right moment to make his presentation, but it seemed that moment never came. Just when it was time to get serious, someone else would show up and Peter had to put off making his offer to sell, but he knew the right time would come.

The possible buyer Peter had in mind was Mr. George Rempel. He was an older man and like most others in the community, he too was a farmer. Mr. Rempel had done well financially in the community and Peter respected him.

Peter had sold Mr. Rempel some farm equipment in the past and knew he had a good net worth. It was time to get serious; Peter didn't have an appointment, but he decided to drive over to the Rempel household and talk to him about buying his businesses and other assets.

Parking his truck in the driveway, Peter went and knocked on the door. George Rempel was not at home; he was on the tractor and working in the field. Peter knew where the field was located and decided to go and pay him a visit.

Driving down the village road, as he neared the location, encircled by dust, he could make out the form of a man on a tractor. Peter was going to wait for him to come to the road, but then decided he would walk out onto the field to see him.

He had never made a sales call like this before. But he had also never been more determined. As he neared the tractor, the farmer saw Peter approaching. Shutting off the engine, he jumped off the tractor, reached out and shook Peter's hand. This was no time for small talk. Both of them knew this was an important meeting.

"Mr. Rempel," Peter said, "you know I have talked about moving back to Canada. I want you to know Sara and I are serious about it and have made our decision; we are definitely going to leave Mexico. You and I have also talked about the possibility of you buying me out. Mr. Rempel, I am ready to sell everything I own in Mexico to you."

It caught Mr. Rempel by surprise! He had never been in a situation like this before. He knew Peter had come on business and was asking him to make a decision. After an awkward moment of silence, Mr. Rempel finally asked, "How much are you asking?" That was the right question, and Peter was ready with the answer.

"I want to make a package deal," Peter said. "The property, the farm equipment inventory, the hardware store and the house should be worth at least three hundred and fifty thousand dollars."

A shrewd buyer, Rempel said, "That is way too much money. I could never pay that high of a price."

"What would you consider to be a good price," Peter asked? Again there was an awkward pause. "One hundred and seventy five thousand dollars," was Rempel's reply. Peter stuck out his hand. "Sold," he said. "I am willing to sell you what we have at just 50 cents on the dollar." Slowly George Rempel reached out and shook Peter's hand; it was a done deal.

Peter knew that he had sold out too cheap. But then, sometimes you have to sacrifice what you have, to get something that you really want. He still had the oven business to dispose of. Peter had kept that out of the deal, since he already had another buyer for it.

When Sara heard about Peter's liquidation sale, she was happy. The planned move they were making would be a new beginning for her and Peter. There were old habits and hurts they were going to leave behind. They were also going to face some new challenges.

At "fifty cents on the dollar," Peter and Sara Thiessen were learning to walk by faith, step by step, one day at a time.

Sara Says Yes!
It Was Time to Leave Mexico

It was 1979; in recent years many of the Mennonites from Mexico had returned to Manitoba and found gainful employment. Some of the government benefits, including Canadian family allowance, as well as old age pension were also appealing. With roots in Canada, for some of them it was not difficult to qualify for the benefits.

The first time Peter Thiessen came to Canada had been 1970, and it was not for any of those reasons. He had come to work and possibly even start a business. Of course there had been the "church factor," and that had worked out well when Peter and Sara first got married.

Sara had not enjoyed the experience of living in Canada. The cold weather, learning to be housewife and then a young mother, and having no really close friends had all added to her frustrations.

She was still amazed that Peter had been willing to return to Mexico just to please her.

What was it that now made Sara willing to leave Mexico? She had a large family and close friends there, and she liked the warm climate in the land where she had been born. Why was she ready to go back up north and endure the cold winters of Winkler, Manitoba? It was not an easy question to answer and certainly had not been an easy decision to make. So why had Sara said, "Yes!"

First off, she had a commitment to her husband Peter that was stronger than any other ties she had. Sara had seen him hurt by some of the leaders of the Church. Maybe they had the right motives, but they surely were not using the right methods in dealing with him.

Then, Peter had been involved in business with some of their family members. Most of the time partnerships are not a good idea. It is too easy to have misunderstandings. Not everyone involved was willing to work as hard as Peter did. That opens the door for blame game; "You are expecting too much," or "You are putting the business before your family."

Peter loved his family as much as anyone else did. But he also enjoyed doing business. It was in his blood. Many of the people he worked with had a better education than he did, but he had a lot more drive than most others. That is what was giving him the leadership skills that he displayed.

Something was also happening to Sara personally. She had always been mature for her age, physically. But during the years she had also been growing emotionally as well as spiritually. Part of it may have come from the years she spent in Canada. She had seen and experienced things most of the other women in the village in Mexico did not understand.

There was also the issue of transportation. Sara's family members, including her sisters, at that time still drove with a horse and buggy. Peter and Sara owned a couple of trucks and a nice car.

Sara even had obtained her own driver's license. It wasn't that Sara tried to show off, but driving a car or truck beat a horse and buggy any day of the week.

Peter had told her that some of the women in the village were jealous; not just her family members, but other women in the community as well. Why was Sara dressing differently and why was she driving a car? She was not abiding by the rules of the Church. Was Peter right? Were they concerned about her faith, or were they envious?

Perhaps it was a little of both. Also, it could be that they did not have the nerve to make the changes that Sara had made. But then, she was married to Peter Thiessen! That may have been Sara's biggest challenge. She hated it when other people, who really did not know or understand her husband, criticized him.

Before Peter and Sara made the decision to move again, they had talked a lot. The first years in their marriage, Peter made most of the hard decisions, but he was changing. He really wanted Sara to be happy, wherever they lived, and she knew it. Her opinion was important to him, and he really was trying to listen.

Another thing that helped Sara make the decision to move back to Canada was her mother. After her husband had passed away, she and her son Ben had moved to Canada. Sara knew when she got back to Winkler; Mom would be waiting for her.

Peter had sold all the fixed assets. He had made a deal for fifty cents on the dollar. He had also sold the oven business. It didn't take him long to pack. All he needed was pants, shirts, shorts and socks, and oh yes, Peter always had to take his hat. He couldn't forget that.

Moving to another country never is easy. What do you take with you and what do you leave behind? There were no garage sales in Mexico so you had to sell things privately. Then Sara found another outlet; it was a community auction.

Even if the prices at the auction were low, Sara felt good about someone else getting a bargain from what she had her left over. It was certainly better than throwing things away.

As time came to leave for Canada they had to get rid of everything that would not fit into the back of the truck camper. What they could not sell, Peter and Sara gave away.

Peter wanted a new vehicle to make the long trip north. But bringing a truck into Canada that was purchased in Mexico was not easy. Instead, Peter made a trip to El Paso, Texas and bought a new Chevy pickup with a shell camper on the back. One more trip to Cuauhtémoc, Mexico to pick up his family and they would be on their way to Canada.

Peter and Sara were husband and wife; they were father and mother of four children, and they were of the same mind and knew what they wanted.

When they got to Winkler, Manitoba, first they would find a house for their family. Then Peter would start a manufacturing company. He had the money to do it. They would create products, and whatever it would be, Peter knew he could sell it.

Traveling with four small children is never easy. Feeding crying babies and changing diapers is never easy, especially in the back of a pickup camper. After several days on the road, Peter and Sara were happy to see the "Welcome To Canada" Customs sign. It was their port of entry at Emerson, Manitoba.

This was well before "Homeland Security" rules were in effect. Crossing the border into Canada should be relatively easy. This time it was not so. Peter had no problem; he had his Canadian Passport. But Sara and two of their four children had been born in the Country of Mexico.

"How long would they stay in Canada; was Sara going to be employed; who would support them while they were here?" The questions from the customs officer kept on coming. It scared Sara!

But leave it to Peter, he was the salesman. It wasn't long and the Canadian Customs officer gave them the green light to go.

Just about thirty more miles into Canada and they would be in Winkler. It seemed a little strange to Sara, but she was actually excited about being back. She was looking forward to seeing the few friends she had left behind when they had moved away seven years ago. Of course, her mother and Ben, would also be waiting for them when they got there.

Within days of their arrival, they had found a house they liked. It was another new beginning. They brought little more than the clothes on their backs so for Sara, it was an enjoyable time. She went shopping a lot. Furniture, dishes, appliances and everything else a household might need, she bought it all.

At the same time, Peter was busy, meeting people, discussing business ideas and looking for the right property to launch his new business. To Peter Thiessen, it was a new world of opportunity.

No longer would he be selling only to Mennonites. Now Western Canada was his market, and the United States was next door. He didn't know it yet, but one day the USA would become his biggest and best customer.

If We Confess Our Sins

He is Faithful and Just to Forgive Us

It seemed like the only time Peter and Sara got to go back to Mexico was when there was a death in the family. Jake Thiessen, Peter's father, had passed away in 1979. Now another death had happened; this time in 1980. It was the funeral of John Rempel, Peter's step father.

Peter's mother had remarried shortly after Jake Thiessen passed away. She just didn't like the idea of living alone and wanted a man in the house. Now burying her second husband within two years, Peter felt that his mother needed him to be there for the funeral.

There was also some other unfinished business Peter wanted to take care of in Mexico. This was a trip Peter really wanted to make by himself. When Peter arrived in Mexico it was already the day of his step-father's funeral and the village where his family lived was bustling with activity.

His mother let him know how much she appreciated his coming from Canada. Peter had planned to be at the funeral later that afternoon, but it was not to be.

The local Church elders had different plans. Peter had been excommunicated by the Church leadership. Just because there was a death in the family; it did not change his status.

While the rest of the family members were gathered around the casket to show their last respects, Peter was asked not to join them. According to the church rules, he had to keep his distance and sit by himself, outside in the church yard.

Strange as it might seem, Peter was not offended. He did not appreciate the way that Church leadership was treating him, but he knew it was partly his fault and he wanted to make it right. The day after the funeral Peter asked for a meeting with the Church elders.

When he had asked to transfer his membership from the Church in Canada, he had made a promise to the Church in Mexico. He had agreed to abide by the rules and regulations of the Church, knowing full well he would not do it. To Peter that was a lie and he wanted to ask them for their forgiveness.

Secondly, before he was received into the Church as a member in good standing, they had asked him if there was any "sin" in his life that he had not confessed to God and to the Church elders. Again he had lied. There was something he was not willing to acknowledge and confess openly. But this time, he wanted to be completely honest with them.

Although Peter and the Church leaders did not agree on whether certain behavior was right or wrong, each of them understood what it meant to be honest. Peter had bared his heart to them and they in turn, had offered him their forgiveness. That was all Peter needed. He was ready to go back to Canada. A spiritual load he had carried for a long time had been lifted.

The trip to Mexico and the experience with the Church leaders had impacted Peter. More than ever, he wanted to be honest with everyone and everything he did. This was true in his business dealings as well as his personal life and especially in his relationship with his wife Sara.

The very thing he had hidden from the Church leaders, he had also kept secret from his Sara. He had not committed murder and was not a fugitive from the law. To others it might not have looked like a big deal. But to Peter it had become an issue between him and God and he was going to deal with it.

He had talked to God about it many times before. He was sure that God had forgiven him for his wrongdoings when he confessed them, but this was different.

In his heart, he knew he needed to tell Sara about it but he didn't want to do it. How would she react? No, he had not been unfaithful to her and there was not another person involved. Still it kept haunting him.

Driving back home from Mexico, it gave Peter time to think. He also had time to pray. He asked God for strength and for wisdom. He wanted to do the right thing but also at the right time. He was going to talk to Sara as soon as he got back home to Winkler.

The kids were happy to see him and Sara was glad he had a safe trip. After a bit of small talk, Peter decided, "This is the time." "Sara," he began, "there is something I want to tell you.

As he began to talk to her, he could see the frustration in her eyes. She had heard enough and didn't want any more of the details. "I cannot forgive you," she shouted. "I am going to leave you."

In anger she rushed out of the house, slamming the back door behind her. Sara didn't know where she was going; she just wanted to get away. As she stepped out into the backyard, suddenly, within a hundred feet of where she was standing, a bolt of lightning struck the ground in front of her.

It was way too close for comfort and it had her full attention. Suddenly Sara heard a voice. "If you don't forgive Peter, I cannot forgive you." Whether it was an audible voice or just in her heart, she knew it was God speaking directly to her and there was no doubt, Sara got the message.

She had an immediate change of heart. Spinning around, Sara headed back into the house. There was Peter, still on his knees praying. When she saw him, with tears in her eyes, she said, "Yes, Peter, I forgive you, and please forgive me for not forgiving you!"

Because of the shed blood of Jesus, when he died for the sins of mankind on the cross of Calvary; what Peter had confessed to God and that night confessed to his wife Sara, is under the blood; forgiven and not to be remembered anymore.

With tears flowing down their faces and arms wrapped around each other, Peter and Sara embraced. They loved each other more than ever before! More than just the love of husband for his wife; it was a demonstration of the love of God.

1 John 1:9 says it well; "If we confess our sin, He is faithful and just to forgive our sin, and to cleanse us from all unrighteousness."

This was a spiritual turning point in Peter's life. He felt like a new man, totally clean on the inside. No longer could Satan, the accuser remind him of his past. He decided to let Jesus answer the door the next time the devil came knocking.

Now, many years later Peter will still tell you, "If you want to do business God's way, begin by being honest with God, and if you are married, be honest with your spouse."

Peter in The Slammer
Accused of Stealing His Own Car

Peter Thiessen was confident he had enough capital to begin a new business in Canada. He had sold all their assets in Mexico at fifty cents on the dollar, and still came out with about $200,000 cash.

That is what Peter and Sara had in hand when they rolled into Winker Manitoba in their brand new Chevy pickup truck. Not bad for a guy who had left Canada just five years earlier with about $20,000 in his pocket.

But then he had also owned an almost new Barracuda. That was the car he had sold for $1,800 and then bought the horse and buggy for $1,900. Now it was just a distant memory,

Having worked in Winkler Manitoba, for almost four years, Peter had some good business contacts. Also, he knew numerous other families who had moved back to Canada from Mexico, who might be good potential employees for the business he was planning to begin.

On highway 32, three miles south of Winkler was a nice housing development. It was a well treed area with newer homes that were selling at a good price. This was Peter's first order of business; he would purchase a house for their growing family. He found a house that both he and Sara liked. They paid forty eight thousand dollars cash for the home and had a clear title to the property.

Peter left the decorating, the purchase of furniture and appliances and other things that the house needed, up to Sara. With a pocketful of cash, this was an assignment any woman would enjoy. Sara had her mother living nearby in the town of Winkler, so Mom and Sara did a lot of shopping together.

Peter did not have an office for his business meetings, so he spent a lot of time at the coffee shops in the area. Living in a cold country with long winters, coffee shops were frequented by most farmers. Here they discussed farming techniques, compared the value of tractors and machinery, and yes, they even talked politics.

Getting to know the area farmers better, Peter got new ideas as to what kind of equipment these farmers might need to improve their farming operation. He wondered, "What could he invent that would make working on the farm easier and more productive?"

Manitoba was home to several Hutterite Colonies. The closest colony was just five miles from Winkler. In their faith and in their life style, there were some characteristics that Old Colony Mennonites and Hutterites had in common.

The big difference was that Hutterites practiced communal living. But Hutterites also had the reputation of being some of the best farmers in the entire province. They owned some of the latest equipment and were committed to the improvement of farming methods. Some of the younger Hutterites also had a creative genius aptitude.

Peter had heard about an aftermarket truck bumper the Hutterites had designed. It was almost a novel idea. The concept was to remove the back truck bumper and replace it with a bumper made out of airtight steel tubing. Connected to the truck air conditioning compressor, the bumper became a mobile air tank.

No need to replace flat tires on the field anymore. Now they could simply use the attached hose to inflate tires and perform dozens of other useful tasks. There was no patent on the idea, so Peter saw it as something he could manufacture and sell to area farmers at a good profit.

Peter decided to start a new business. He called the company **COMSTAR**. The first piece of farm equipment Peter decided to produce was a **SWATH ROLLER**. It was a simple apparatus, pulled behind any grain swather. It compressed the fresh cut swaths and made them more resistant to wind damage. It was a great idea and soon Peter had a distributor and his first order, for a product he had not yet produced.

Going home to his new house that night, Peter was excited. He told Sara about the order for the 500 **SWATH ROLLERS** that he had received. It was well over two hundred thousand dollars. Obviously they were a happy family looking forward to building their new business.

Getting the order was the fun part. Now the **SWATH ROLLERS** had to be manufactured. In a short time Peter had found the property he needed to build his factory. It was at the edge of town on Airport Road, located next to the Winkler Airport. Cash in hand, he bought the property at a good price.

Within just six months the 40 by 60 steel building was finished. An investment of another $60,000 and Peter had all the equipment he needed to start manufacturing. With three other employees, Peter was able to fill the **SWATH ROLLER** order on time. During the first year of the new business they had grossed annual sales exceeding $250,000.

With the coming of the New Year, it was time to get into the
Air Tank Bumper business. They would need new equipment
and more raw materials as well as additional employees, so Peter
went to see his local banker. When he returned he had established
a line of credit of $115,000 and the **Air Tank Bumper** concept
was put in motion.

Back to the coffee shop; Peter met a businessman who had been
the John Deere dealer in the area. Now he was in the implement
cab business. Canada has cold spring and fall days, so a cab on a
tractor or any other self propelled machinery made good sense.

He already had dealers across western Canada and made a
proposal to Peter. "You make the **Air Tank Bumpers** and let
me sell them for you." It made good sense to him. Here was an
established distributor with good connections. Why duplicate the
selling effort? Peter came back to his **Comstar** business excited.
Now he had a verbal order for a thousand **Air Tank Bumpers** to
add to the five hundred **Swath Rollers** order.

"This could be the beginning of something big," Peter thought.
Investing the last of his operating capital, he ordered the steel and
other components that he needed to fill the order. By the spring
of 1983, there were 1,000 **Air Tank Bumpers** and 500 **Swath
Rollers** on the **Comstar** property ready for delivery to his new
farm equipment distributors.

Then Peter Thiessen got a phone call; it was a bad call. One of
the new equipment distributors was on the line. "I can't take the
bumpers," he began. "Interest rates are too high, and dealers are
cutting back," he continued. "But you gave me your word, and I
have invested heavily to fill your order, surely you are not serious!"
Peter said. As Peter was soon going to find out, the distributor was
very serious.

Always the optimist, Peter thought, "I am sure that I can sell
the **Air Tank Bumpers** myself." But time was not on his side, and
apparently neither was the bank. Talk about high interest. This was

the 1980s. Suddenly the rate on his business line of credit shot up past the 30% mark. "That should be illegal," Peter said to himself.

Peter sensed that something bad was going to happen. When he talked to the banker about his situation with the distributor, he didn't get much help. Both Peter and the banker knew that he was out of operating money and his request for an increase in the line of credit was rejected.

The only thing the banker did not have as collateral on the bank note was the house that Peter and Sara owned. It was free and clear of any financial encumbrances. The banker said, "Peter, bring me the title to your house, and I can increase your line of credit."

Without even giving it a second thought Peter said, "No!" This was an agreement Peter and Sara had made. They would never risk the home they lived in, for the sake of the business.

It was March 29, 1984, eight o'clock in the morning. Peter was at the **COMSTAR** office, trying to unlock the door, but the key would not work. Suddenly it dawned on him, "The bank had taken possession of **COMSTAR**. His business was closed."

COMSTAR was in legal receivership. Just three years ago they had come from Mexico with $200,000 cash. Now it was all gone and he did not know what to do next. Peter's thoughts turned to the survival of his family. When he told Sara what had happened, she was at the point of panic! "What are we going to do now?" was her big question.

Before the Christmas of 1983, Peter had visited the local Chrysler dealership in Morden, Manitoba. Business had been good in the past year and he wanted to surprise Sara. He wrote the check and purchased a brand new, silver Chrysler New Yorker as a Christmas gift for her. It was beautiful and had all of the latest bells and whistles.

Sara's new car was in the driveway. What he did not realize; he had given his personal guarantee to the bank and the car was part of the bank's collateral. In a matter of hours the car was seized and locked up in the local Ford dealership.

The Courts had already appointed a receiver to handle the legal liquidation of COMSTAR and Peter had already talked to him. Not having retained a lawyer, Peter asked the receiver about his legal rights. "All the company assets, including the bank accounts are frozen," was his response.

"What about the AIR TANK BUMPERS stored in the United States? Who do they belong to," Peter asked. The receiver told him that anything outside of Canada was not under the Court's jurisdiction. That gave Peter an idea. COMSTAR had a product distributor in the United States and they had shipped 24 AIR TANK BUMPERS that were not yet paid for.

Without telling anyone besides Sara, Peter made a trip to North Dakota to pick up the unsold inventory. Right now, the welfare of Sara and his four children was his biggest concern. He could sell the bumpers at a discount and generate some immediate cash.

This was only the beginning of the nightmare. That night someone had broken into the Ford dealership and stolen the Chrysler New Yorker. The first suspect; it was Peter Thiessen. The Winkler police chief was alerted about the theft. The result was a warrant for the arrest of Peter Thiessen.

Peter was on the highway, back to Winkler when he saw a flashing red light behind him. When he pulled over, the next thing he knew, he was in handcuffs and being accused of breaking into the local Ford dealership and stealing the Chrysler New Yorker.

The next stop was the local Winkler Jail. Peter was locked up for the night but the game was not over. The arresting officer called Sara. He told her that Peter was in jail, charged with car theft.

He continued to tell her that Peter had already confessed to the crime. Sara knew it was not true. Her response was, "That cannot be my husband." She knew he had been out of town. She also knew Peter was not a thief.

The interrogation continued; "Mr. Thiessen, we just spoke to your wife. She admitted that you broke into the Ford dealership and took the car," the officer lied. Peter knew it was not the truth. In his heart Peter believed that somehow they would make it through this horrible ordeal.

Without a confession from Peter and with no other evidence, the police chief released him the next day. When Peter finally got home he had a phone call from the bank saying. "If you bring in your house title, we can increase your line of credit." Peter was suspicious, but this was his last hope. He and Sara agreed, they were willing to take the chance.

As Peter's mind began to clear, he realized that what had happened to him and **COMSTAR** might have been legal in Mexico, but surely not in Canada. He knew about Harry Walsh, a lawyer in Winnipeg. He was one of the toughest lawyers in Canada and Peter wanted to meet with him.

When Walsh heard Peter's story he became indignant. Handing his card to Peter he said, "Take this card back to Winkler and give it to the banker. Ask them if they want to deal with you or with me." There was no fee for the consultation. If there would be a lawsuit it would be on a basis of a contingency agreement.

Leaving the lawyer's office, Peter felt better; still he had a lot of problems to solve. Would they be able to stay in Canada? Could he rescue his business from the grasp of legal receivership?

Would Sara be able to understand what had happed to them? "God," Peter prayed, "I need your help." Give me the strength to keep going and to do what is right."

Peter was angry. He knew what the Banker and the Winkler Police Officer had done was wrong. He decided to take the advice the lawyer Walsh had given him. He decided to visit the bank one more time.

When he presented the card to the Banker, he noticed an immediate change in his attitude. The Banker may have thought he was dealing with an uneducated Mexican Mennonite, who had moved back to Canada. What he didn't know was that this Mexican Mennonite had good connections.

According to Canadian law, likely the bank did not have a legal right to include Peter Thiessen's home in the receivership action, but they had done it anyway. Now the bank was offering to sell the house back to Peter and Sara if they would sign a note for $40,000 with an interest rate of just 8%.

They needed a place to live, so it was better than nothing. Peter and Sara agreed and signed the agreement. At least they would have a roof over their heads. The receivership auction was still about 60 days out. It was a dark night when Peter decided to go back to the **COMSTAR** business location. He was there with a big truck he had borrowed.

He began loading the **AIR TANK BUMPERS** and hauling them away. He was headed for his mother's house, 10 miles out of town. He buried them under a pile of hay bales. This was a big undertaking, but by morning the "bumper move" was complete.

When Sara saw what Peter had done, she was not pleased. "What are you going to tell the court appointed receiver," she wanted to know. He didn't have an answer. He knew he couldn't lie, so reluctantly he loaded the bumpers back on the truck, and returned them to **COMSTAR**. The only difference; he returned them in broad daylight.

What a hectic week it had been. **COMSTAR** was locked up and in legal court receivership, his bank account was frozen, Sara's car had been seized, Peter had spent a night in jail, they had lost their home; what else could possibly go wrong?

Peter counted his assets. He had exactly $7.76 in his pocket. That was it. Then he remembered, he still had a full container of paint thinners in his possession. It was not on the court receiver's list, so Peter had the right to sell it.

Peter thought that Isaac Loewen, his earlier employer at the **LOADMASTER COMPANY,** might want to purchase the thinners and decided to go and take it to him. Peter was right. Mr. Loewen wanted the product and agreed to his $80 price.

But then he reminded Peter that he had an outstanding bill of $69.00 with **LOADMASTER.** Taking the paint thinners, he gave Peter $11.00 cash as the final settlement for the sale.

This was not what Peter had expected. Adding the $11.00 to his $7.76; Peter now had $18.76. It was barely enough to feed his family for a couple of days.

"God, I need your help," Peter prayed. He discovered that God can answer short prayers. The answer to his prayer would come through a new idea.

Note:

Twenty years after this unlawful act by the Winkler Chief of Police, the Mayor of the City of Winkler, Manitoba issued a letter of apology to Peter and Sara Thiessen for the wrongful arrest and the misconduct of the arresting Officer.

In September of 2011, Peter and Sara Thiessen made a donation of $50,000 to the City of Winkler, Manitoba for the Bethel Heritage Park. See the picture in the photo section.

Starting Over with $7.76
Big Dream – Small Beginning

Shortly after his company, COMSTAR had been ordered into bank receivership, Peter went to see Diedrich Dyck, Sara's brother. Having been brothers-in-law for over twelve years, they knew each other well.

Peter really wasn't looking for any advice; he simply needed someone with a listening ear and Diedrich was willing to make himself available. It was always enjoyable to listen to Peter and discover what his next big business plan was going to be.

This time it seemed different. Peter was much more serious and Diedrich could see that he was worried. The big question Peter kept asking was, "What do I do now? Should he forget about business and simply get a job? Was it time to leave Winkler and move back to Mexico? Was there any way that he could start another business in Winker?" These were not questions for Diedrich; they were questions Peter was asking himself.

Somehow "Getting a job," did not appeal to Peter. He much preferred being in business for himself. Here was the problem; at the moment he had no money and no collateral. Peter had enough banking experience to know that you can't start a new business without any capital.

He also knew that you can't borrow money without pledged assets; unless you have a co-signer. "That's it;" Peter thought to himself. "I can get a co-signer to help me start the business."

Diedrich Dyck had never been in business and did not see himself as a businessman. His net worth was small and sometimes he had struggled to just feed his family. But Diedrich had a small line of credit at the Winkler Credit Union and he told Peter about it.

It was just $5,000, but he was willing to make it available to Peter Thiessen. Suddenly Diedrich saw a smile on Peter's face. He knew Peter had an idea and he couldn't hide it. "Diedrich," he began, "Let's go into business together. We will be 50/50 partners. We can start with your $5,000 line of credit and I will come up with another $5,000."

Through the years Diedrich had watched Peter Thiessen, and somehow he believed that Peter was going to build another profitable business. If he became a partner with Peter, maybe he would be able to improve his own lot in life as well.

With nothing but a handshake, Diedrich Dyck and Peter Thiessen became business partners. The new company was going to be named **ALLSTAR**.

Thinking about starting another business was exciting to Peter. Suddenly he had new energy. Still there was unfinished business from the past that had to be taken care of. This included the **COMSTAR** business liquidation auction. On the announced day of the auction, Peter and his new business partner arrived early.

They heard the voice of the auctioneer; "The auction will begin in 15 minutes," he said. "You will need a number to be able to bid.

If you have not yet registered, go to the clerk and pick up your bidding number."

Peter still felt the pain of losing everything he had worked so hard to achieve, but he was willing to put that behind him. He had a new company, a new business partner and some great new product ideas. He was ready for the auction to begin. No one else at the auction knew the value of the **COMSTAR** inventory and equipment as well as Peter did.

He had bought each welder and every other piece of equipment that would be sold today. He had paid cash for it; now he wanted to buy it back one more time. At the close of the auction, with just $5,000, they had been able to purchase well over $50,000 in welders and other manufacturing equipment. That was just 10¢ on the dollar and Peter liked those odds.

Now their new company had manufacturing equipment, but what kind of machinery were they going to manufacture? Peter had already done some research. He had visited local farm equipment dealers and regional distributors to see what kind of agricultural equipment was selling well. He was looking for a product idea they could improve and manufacture under their own brand name.

There was one specific item that had Peter's interest. It was a **DRILL FILL TANK**. Every farmer owned a seeding drill. Without it, there was no way to get the seed into the ground. But filling the drill boxes was time consuming and could be wasteful, when the seed boxes overflowed.

The **DRILL FILL TANK** was the answer to the problem. There already was some similar equipment on the market, but with a little improvement, Peter and Diedrich knew they could create and manufacture a better product.

Peter never was afraid of competition. In his opinion, when you have to compete for a sale, it only makes you do a better job. His philosophy; "Improve your product and your service and you will likely get the business."

Although Peter Thiessen and Diedrich Dyck were 50/50 business partners, Peter had not yet come up with his share of the investment capital. He needed $5,000 to match Diedrich's $5,000 line of credit at the Credit Union.

Peter didn't know how or where he would find the operating capital for the business, but he was sure it was going to come. All he needed to do was look for it. More important than $5,000, he had a heart full of faith and a positive attitude. Peter Thiessen had bounced back.

Rich Man and Lazarus

Tycoon Gets the Message

Peter and Sara had survived the impossible and already things were beginning to look up. He had a new product idea they could manufacture that farmers needed. Peter knew how to sell; and selling creates cash flow. But he also knew that it takes money to make money

Peter was well aware that people in the community were talking about him. When someone is in trouble, people seem to enjoy doing that. It would have been easier to just stay at home, but Peter forced himself to go to the local coffee shop. That is also where the town gossips gathered.

There was a businessman living in the community most everybody knew. Beginning as a farmer, he had become a real estate tycoon. Although his net worth was private, it was well known that he was wealthy. There was something else folks knew about him, he was tight with his money.

The tycoon and Peter were only casual acquaintances, but for some reason he seemed to enjoy visiting with Peter. With **Comstar** in receivership, Peter knew going to the bank for credit was useless; it would only waste his time. He decided to give the tycoon a call.

Getting an appointment with him was not hard. But getting money from him was a different story. As they met at the tycoon's home, Peter began to explain what had happened to him in the past 30 days. He was careful and tried to tell it just like it had happened.

Hearing himself tell this intriguing story, some of the things seemed hard for even Peter to believe, but he knew they were true. Now it was time to talk about the future and Peter already had a plan. It was not in writing, but Peter had it down pat.

He had a manufacturing idea for a good product. He was sure he could produce and sell it and make a good profit. All he needed was the operating capital to get the business started. Having lived on the farm, the tycoon could see the value of the proposed **Drill Fill Tanks.**

As he finished his presentation, he looked the tycoon in the eye. Peter said, "Sir, would you be willing to lend me $5,000? That's all I need to begin this new business; just $5,000." Without hesitation, he gave Peter an answer; the answer was, "No!"

"How could a man who bragged about making thousands of dollars on the stock market in less than a day, be so stingy," Peter wondered. In just a few days the tycoon called Peter back. This time he had a plan.

He would lend the $5,000 to Peter, but there was a condition attached. He asked Peter to bring the clear titles to the homes that both Peter's and Sara's mothers owned. He wanted them as collateral for the loan.

It was an insult. Peter told him there was no way that he would get his family involved in his financial affairs. Peter asked the tycoon for one more meeting. He had a point he wanted to make.

The day they met, Peter did most of the talking. He had something that he wanted to say. Rather than discussing business ideas or financing, Peter began with a Bible story.

"Do you know the story of the rich man and Lazarus?" he asked. "You are the **Rich Man** and I am Lazarus." Peter continued "You brag about how easy it is to make money, but you won't even give me the crumbs from your table. That's all I am asking, just crumbs, but still, you won't do it."

"Do you know what happened to the **Rich Man?**" Peter asked? "He died and went to hell. Is that where you want to go?" His theology may not have been right, but Peter definitely was getting his point across. As they parted, Peter felt sure this was the end of a friendly relationship and certainly, he would not get any money out of this tight wad.

That night, at 4:00 AM, Peter received a phone call. It was the tycoon calling. "Is this Peter Thiessen?" He began. "I can't sleep. Last night when my son came into the house I was still wide awake."

"Dad, why aren't you asleep?" He asked me." 'I told him that it was Peter Thiessen. I then told my son what you had said about the story of the **Rich Man** and Lazarus, and that your words were keeping me awake.'

'My son replied, 'Dad, I think maybe Peter is right. Why don't you lend him the money?'" The tycoon concluded "Peter, can you meet me at the house in the morning?"

Peter could hardly believe his ears. Was this the same man he had talked to just hours earlier? "I will see you there," was Peter's response; what else could he say? The tycoon told him not to be there before 10:00 AM. "Now I am going to bed to get some sleep," he said.

Peter doesn't like being late. At 9:55 next morning he was at the house. Sitting down at the table, the tycoon said, "Peter, explain your plan one more time."

Peter was impatient; he had already given him the details of his new business idea, twice before. What he didn't know was that the tycoon had been taking notes of each of their previous meetings.

Once again Peter talked about the business he was going to build and why he needed the $5,000. The tycoon responded, "I am not going to lend you the $5,000 you are asking for." Peter was ready to explode. "He must be crazy," he thought to himself. The tycoon continued, "Peter, you could not tell the same detailed story to me three times, if it were not the truth. I believe you."

"Here is what we are going to do. You and I are going to go to the **Credit Union** and I will help you set up a line of credit for your business. It will not be for $5,000, but for $180,000. That is what you will need to build the new business that you talked to me about."

Peter was overwhelmed. He did not know what to say. Was he hearing right? Was it possible that this businessman, whom Peter had seen as a "tight wad," could be the man God would use to answer his prayer? Peter lost no time and within hours he, his partner and his "angel" signed on the dotted line at the **Credit Union.** Peter Thiessen was back in business.

For the record, Peter and his business partner Diedrich Dyck had entered into an agreement with the tycoon. They agreed they would split the profits from the new business three ways. One third would go to each of the partners and the remaining third would go to the Tycoon.

That night, as Peter usually did, he took time to pray. He thanked God for hearing and answering his prayer. He also remembered to pray for the **"Rich man"** God had used to help Peter establish his needed line of credit. "God," he prayed, "Please let my rich friend have a good sleep tonight."

Looking back on this valuable lesson, Peter realized that although the tycoon may have been "tight with his money," he became a generous man when he believed that God was telling him what to do.

Peter did not know it at the time, but there was going to be a day when he would be considered the **"Rich man."** He too would need to make the decisions of where to invest and when to say, "No."

Ask Peter what gave him the audacity to approach "the tycoon" for $5,000 and he will tell you, "It just seemed like the right thing to do." Learning to hearing God's voice and walking by faith is a process that comes with experience. For Peter, this was part of the learning process.

More than sheer audacity, the Bible talks about God giving a "gift of faith," to an individual. Peter may well have been using that gift without even being aware of it. Secondly, the "favor of God," can open doors that we could never open by our human effort. That was certainly the case with Peter and "the tycoon."

It is important to recognize that walking by faith will be different for each individual. The principles are the same, but how they are applied may differ from Peter Thiessen and his unusaul business experiences.

Ready – Set – Grow!
Nothing Happens Without Selling

As a businessman, Peter knew that everything depends on selling. You can have wonderful ideas and great products, but before there can be any profits, somebody has to be able to sell the manufactured goods.

He remembered the **AIR TANK BUMPER** fiasco that they had experienced. **COMSTAR** had failed because an equipment distributor did not follow through on promised performance. Peter surely didn't want to repeat that experience.

Southern Manitoba is called **GARDEN VALLEY**. Even today the majority of the farmers come from a Mennonite background. Rich soil and good growing conditions have made it part of the "Bread Basket" of Canada and Winkler Manitoba is in the heart of the "Bread Basket."

Surrounded by productive farmland and prospering farms, there are many other related industries in Southern Manitoba.

Within 75 miles of Winkler, Peter had heard of an aggressive equipment distributor, and he wanted to meet him.

The distributor had already been selling **DRILL FILL TANKS.** When he saw the new **ALLSTAR** improved version, it was love at first sight. He knew he could sell them across Canada. The **DRILL FILL TANKS** were priced at $2,500 each. He gave Peter an order for 100 units. That was $250,000, and this was just his first sales call. Peter's visit had paid off.

With such a substantial cash deposit in his pocket, Peter's entrepreneurial spirit was rising and Diedrich his partner, shared the excitement. He could hardly wait to get home and tell Sara about his success. Of course he also wanted to call the tycoon. Peter wanted him to know that the business idea he had repeated three times, was really working.

ALLSTAR already had **DRILL FILL TANK** orders, they had the manufacturing equipment and a good line of credit, but they still had no building or location. They needed a sizeable building with adequate electrical wiring to handle the arc welders and other power driven tools, like cutters, saws, drills, lathes and punches.

Then Peter got a welcome phone call. It was from another local businessman, Abe Wiebe. He was calling to make a most unusual offer. He had heard about Peter's problems with **COMSTAR** and the bank. Abe Wiebe had a vacant building and he wanted to make it available to Peter, as the manufacturing facility for his new company, **ALLSTAR.**

"If you make it, you can pay me. If not, I'll take the loss," was his offer. How could Peter refuse? This was just what **ALLSTAR** needed. There was more than enough space. Peter saw it as another answer to prayer from the Heavenly Father, who loves and cares for all of his children. Peter said, "Yes" to Mr. Wiebe, and "Thank you" to God.

Soon the welders were flashing and the shop buzzing with excitement as the first **DRILL FILL TANK** came off the small assembly line. These were not ordinary **DRILL FILL TANKS.** They had the **ALLSTAR** name on them and that meant at the moment, they were the finest available anywhere.

As the first year of business came to a close for **ALLSTAR,** it had been a big success. Even within the first 90 days, Peter had been able to repay the line of credit and reward the tycoon handsomely for his efforts. The company had made a good profit. Both Peter and his partner Diedrich Dyck had a great Christmas with their families. They were looking forward to the next year; it should be even better.

The distributor had already given **ALLSTAR** the next order for 250 **DRILL FILL TANKS.** Everything looked good, but Peter could sense there was a problem. He decided to make a trip to the province of Saskatchewan and visit some of the equipment dealers who were selling the **DRILL FILL TANKS.**

With a sample **ALLSTAR DRILL FILL TANK** on the back of his truck, Peter and his traveling partner Ben Dyck, who was Sara's brother, were heading west. As they pulled into North Battleford, Saskatchewan, Peter spotted one of their **ALLSTAR** distributors and pulled into the equipment lot.

As Peter entered the building, one of the business partners had seen the **ALLSTAR** name on the **DRILL FILL TANK** on the truck. Without even an introduction, he began to read "the riot act," to Peter. There were customers nearby who heard his rant, but that didn't stop him. He wanted Peter to know what kind of a low down scoundrel Peter was.

When Peter returned to the truck, Ben could see something was very wrong. "What happened?" he asked. Peter's only response was "I don't know." He had never seen anyone so angry before. Sitting there quietly, Peter and Ben prayed, asking God for wisdom. Then Peter decided to go back into the business one more time. He needed to know what had been so upsetting to the man.

There was another tirade of words, not fit to be spoken by anyone of decent character. Still, Peter could not figure out what had triggered the verbal outrage he had just heard. At the point of giving up, Dave, the other partner in the business, approached Peter. He tried to explain the reason for the embarrassing outrage they had just experienced.

Here is what had happened. The distributor **Allstar** had in Manitoba had sold **Drill Fill Tanks** to the North Battleford, Saskatchewan equipment dealers at a supposedly wholesale price. Then he went out and sold **Drill Fill Tanks** directly to the farmers in the area, undercutting the dealer price.

Now Peter began to see the picture. While it did not justify the behavior he had just experienced, he could at least understand what had triggered it. Finally it was Peter's turn to talk. "I am not the distributor," Peter said, "I am the owner as well as the manufacturer of **Drill Fill Tanks** and we are going to make things right with you."

To mend the relationship, Peter offered a special price to the dealer, but it was only good for the day. Suddenly Dennis, the "mean mouth," had a change of heart. He understood that he had over re-acted, but "I'm sorry," was not in his vocabulary. Instead, his way of making things right was to give Peter another order for **Drill Fill Tanks.**

Peter reminded Dennis that he wanted a 20% deposit with any order they would give him. "I'll take four," was his immediate response. Now Dave the other partner joined the conversation; "Let's make that eight," he said. Suddenly it looked like an auction sale, with the partners trying to outbid each other on the size of their order.

When the dust settled, they had given Peter an order for 20 **Drill Fill Tanks** and written a check for 20% of the total price as a cash deposit. Leaving North Battleford, Ben could not believe what he heard. Peter was grinning from ear to ear. The Bible talked about loving your enemies. It had worked and Peter had a check to prove it.

The rest of the trip was easy. Going from town to town, Peter and Ben met dealers who liked the **ALLSTAR DRILL FILL TANKS.** They were pleased to meet the owner and were generous with their orders. By the time they returned to Winkler three weeks later, Peter had a half million dollars in purchase orders, and a 20% deposit from each order.

The word was out. **ALLSTAR'S** improved **DRILL FILL TANK** product line was well received. Now it was time to grow. They would need more space, more raw materials and more equipment and obviously, more employees.

They would also have to go to trade shows to advertise their product line to other equipment dealers in Western Canada. Nobody could sell a product better than Peter Thiessen. He liked meeting people and they liked meeting him.

Peter Thiessen is a trusting individual and doesn't keep many secrets. Sara thinks that sometimes he is too trusting. But that is Peter's personality. He enjoys talking about successful experiences. What he didn't know, he had a competitor who was eyeing the growth of **ALLSTAR.**

LODE KING, a farm equipment manufacturer in Winkler also had a **DRILL FILL TANK** they were selling, but it did not have the **ALLSTAR** improvements. Peter knew **LODE KING** was no competition for **ALLSTAR.** He was getting ready to head for the Regina Saskatchewan farm equipment show when something got his attention.

He saw a **LODE KING** truck with drill filling equipment on it. He could see it had the **ALLSTAR** improved features installed. **ALLSTAR** had applied for a patent on the feature and Peter knew **LODE KING** was violating their patent rights.

Confronting the management at **LODE KING,** Peter said, "Take it off." Now aware that **ALLSTAR** had filed for a patent, **LODE KING** complied and removed the ALLSTAR feature, before going to the Regina trades show.

At the Regina show, Peter outsold the competition, five to one. Was it the features of the ALLSTAR equipment, or was it Peter Thiessen's sales ability? No doubt it was a combination of both. It wasn't long after the show, that LODE KING approached ALLSTAR. They were interested in the purchase of the ALLSTAR COMPANY.

Just three years ago Peter had lost everything when COMSTAR went into receivership. He had started over again with limited funds. Now **Lode King,** an established manufacturer wanted to negotiate the purchase of ALLSTAR.

LODE KING was ready to make an offer. They wanted to buy everything; the property, the equipment and the inventory "Peter, how much would it take to buy the ALLSTAR COMPANY?" was LODE KING'S question.

Not one for much detail, Peter said, "We will take $800,000 cash and a new TRIPLE E MOTOR HOME." That seemed like a lot of money, but LODE KING had the cash and they knew they could quickly recover their investment.

With a $50,000.00 down payment it was a done deal. Now all they needed was for the lawyers to create the necessary purchase agreement. It was a great day for Peter and Diedrich, when LODE KING wrote the final check and gave them the keys to their new TRIPLE E MOTOR HOME.

Like kids with a new toy, Peter and Diedrich loaded their families into their new TRIPLE E COACH. As they headed out of Winkler, there were smiles on every face. How did this all happen? No one could really give a good answer. A glance upward and a raised index finger pointing to the sky was Peter's way of saying, "God did it for us."

It seemed like a fairy tale. How could all this have happened in such a short while? Still Peter knew it was true. After all he still lived with the princess. Sara had married him 15 years earlier. It had been for better or for worse. Peter hoped that the worst part was over. He wanted Sara to enjoy the better days ahead.

When you've been out of money and suddenly you have several hundred thousand dollars in hand as your part of the transaction, what do you do with that much cash? That was the question Peter and Diedrich had to answer.

Their accountant made them aware that there can be tax consequences when you sell a business. Peter knew about income tax, but what is capital gains tax? "How much will capital gains tax be?" Peter asked the accountant. When he got the answer, Peter said "Wow! That's a lot of money.

"Is there any way we can avoid paying capital gains?" he asked. The accountant explained that in Canada you have 12 months after the sale of a business or property to reinvest the proceeds and possibly be exempt from capital gains taxes.

Peter liked what he was learning. He enjoyed business, so why not start another company and avoid paying capital gains altogether? The more he thought about it, the better it seemed.

He discussed the idea of starting another new business with his brother-in-law Diedrich. "Think about it," Peter told him, "And then let's talk about it again." Peter knew whatever they chose to do; it would be bigger than anything they had ever done before.

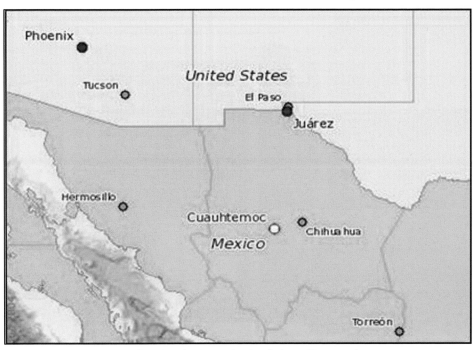

Mennonites from Canada Migrated to Cuauhtémoc, Mexico in the 1920s

Chihuahua State Statue Honoring Mennonite Farmers in Mexico

The House Where Peter Thiessen Lived through His Teenage Years

Made of Sun Dried Clay Bricks, the 85 Year Old House is Still in Use.

The House Where Sara Dyck Thiessen was born - Still Occupied Today

Sara Thiessen and Dorothy Enns Visiting Sara's Childhood Home

Old Colony German Mennonite School - Peter's Only Formal Education

The One Room School Classroom with Slate Chalk Board Writing Tablets

The Old Colony Mennonite Village Church

Peter Thiessen and a John Deere Tractor with Steel Spiked Wheels

From a Black 1968 Plymouth Barracuda to a Horse & Buggy

Peter Going to See Sara?   Old Fashioned Outhouse Still in Use

Original **Comstar** building- Now an Auto Body Repair Shop

Allstar Building Where **Drill Fill Tanks** Were Manufactured

Former **Douglas Manufactruing** Lawn Equipment Plant

PJ Trailers US Headquarters - A Testimony to God's Faithfulness

PJ Trailers Factory, Tigertown, Texas - A Recent Aerial View

A Load of **PJ Trailers** Leaving the Plant in Tigertown, Texas

PJ Trailers, Canada, Inc.

PJ Trailers, Canada, Inc. Headquarters

Peter & Sara Thiessen with Peter & Dorothy Enns in Mexico

Peter & Sara Thiessen & daughter Lisa Presenting a $50,000 Donation to Phil Ens
Back left to right: Winkler City Manager Dave Burgess, Mayor Martin Harder, City Councilor
Ron Neisteter and Bethel Park Committee Chair Bill Siemens. Photo by Allison Friesen, Winkler Times

Peter & Sara Thiessen on Their 40th Wedding Anniversary Celebration

Peter Thiessen, Jr. (The **"P"** in **PJ Trailers**)

Pete & Lisa Thiessen Zacharias, with Lenexa, Selena & Micah

Just the Grandkids

Jake & Judy Thiessen with Latelia, infant Jager & Summer

Frank & Darcy Thiessen with Rori, Logan & Aubrey

Henry & Sarah Thiessen Friesen with Elijah & Kezia

Elijah Ty Friesen
February 21, 2005
July 26, 2011

Let not your heart be
troubled; you believe in God,
believe also in Me.

In My Father's house are many
mansions; if it were not so,
I would have told you. I go
to prepare a place for you.

And if I go and prepare a place
for you, I will come again and
receive you to Myself; that
where I am, there you
may be also. John 14: 1 - 3

God Cares

Who will help us understand,
When things don't go as we had planned?
When one we love is snatched away,
And no one knows, just what to say.
GOD CAN!

Who understands when we've been bruised?
When we are crushed, and feel confused?
When things that happen don't seem fair,
Because we know that He is there,
GOD WILL!

Who can heal a broken heart?
And mend what death has torn apart?
What circumstances would destroy,
Who can turn it into joy?
GOD DOES!

A Tribute to Elijah Friesen

Up in Smoke and No Insurance
The Insurance Company Called it Arson

Peter and Sara Thiessen were enjoying their new life in Winkler, Manitoba. They had a beautiful house, a new car, a pickup truck and money in the bank. To top it off within the past year, a new baby girl had been born into their family. They named her Sarah.

The **ALLSTAR** manufacturing company Peter and Diedrich Dyck started also had done well. They had made a profit for each of the first two years. Then, within the previous six months, they had sold the company to **LODE KING** for $800,000 cash, plus a new **TRIPLE E MOTOR COACH.**

Suddenly Peter and his partner Diedrich found themselves facing a new challenge. They had made money, now they needed to learn how to protect their hard earned assets. In 1986 Canada had a hefty capital gains tax, but they discovered that there was a way to avoid paying this hefty tax.

Their accountant had given them good advice. He said, "Start another similar business and you can save thousands of dollars in taxes." But there was a time limit; you had to reinvest the capital gains profits within the next 12 months. Peter saw the deadline coming and he knew they would have to make a decision in the near future.

Within just a few miles of Winkler, Manitoba, there was a small company that had Peter's interest. It was **Douglas Manufacturing,** owned by Bill Rempel, a local Mennonite businessman. The company was building lawn and garden equipment, including roto-tillers and a new three blade finishing mower under the **Douglas Brand.**

Douglas had created a great product. It was superior in design and performance. What sales the company had, came from satisfied customer referrals. While word of mouth will always be the best means of advertising, in the face of strong competition, by itself it is not enough to establish a new brand.

What the company was lacking was marketing and distribution expertise. **Douglas Manufacturing** needed someone who was aggressive to run the sales and marketing for the company.

They needed Peter Thiessen, but they didn't know who he was or where he lived; at least not yet. On the other hand, Peter had been looking for a new product or possibly even a new company where he could use his entrepreneurial skills.

Wanting to know more about **Douglas Manufacturing,** Peter decided to visit the operation. As he walked into the shop he immediately liked what he saw. The smell of welder's smoke and the clanging and clacking of power punches and drills reminded him of **Allstar**. He felt right at home in that environment.

Peter was confident he could sell **Douglas Roto-tillers,** but he didn't see himself being an employee of the Company. As he talked to Bill Rempel about the **Douglas** business, he realized that Bill was too small in his thinking. Where Bill was talking of hundreds, Peter was thinking of thousands or even millions.

When he got home that night, he called his former business partner, Diedrich Dyck and told him about his visit to **DOUGLAS MANUFACTURING.** Peter suggested that in the near future, he and Diedrich should pay another visit to **DOUGLAS MANUFACTURING** for a meeting with Rempel.

At first Diedrich was hesitant; he had never had it so good. With cash in the bank from the sale of **ALLSTAR,** he was quite content to simply enjoy life. But Peter reminded him that after paying his taxes, without added income Diedrich's days of leisure would soon come to an end.

Peter knew that Diedrich needed a push. "Diedrich," he said, "Maybe we should purchase **DOUGLAS MANUFACTURING.** We could become partners and all work together. Let Rempel design the equipment, you run the manufacturing and I can handle the sales and marketing division."

It was time for another visit. As Peter and Diedrich got out of the truck and entered **DOUGLAS MANUFACTURING,** Diedrich thought, "This place is not as big as Peter described it," but then, he knew that Peter always saw things as a big opportunity. He never saw the glass as half empty; it was always half full.

It was time to talk business, so Peter popped the question. "Bill, would you consider taking us in as partners in **DOUGLAS MANUFACTURING?**" he asked. "You told me you needed operating money as well as help in sales and marketing. Diedrich and I can assist you in both of those areas."

When Bill Rempel started **DOUGLAS MANUFACTURING** he simply wanted to build lawn and garden equipment. Selling the company had never even entered his mind. Peter could see that Bill was not ready to give him an answer. "Think about it," Peter said, "then let's meet again in a couple of days."

The next time they met, Peter had a plan ready. He proposed that they reorganize the company. Peter and Diedrich would put up the cash **DOUGLAS MANUFACTURING** needed to grow the business. The three of them would be shareholders as well as employees of the company.

The way Peter had outlined it; because he and Diedrich would have to provide the operating capital, they would become the majority shareholders. He would handle sales, Diedrich would run the shop and Bill would continue to work in product improvement and in the development of new product ideas.

Weary of the struggle of trying to raise more money for his startup venture, Bill could see the opportunity of having a piece of something much bigger than what he had. He liked the idea of not having to worry about sales. With Diedrich running the shop, Bill would be able to do what he enjoyed doing and was best at; designing new equipment.

Bill made the decision to accept Peter's proposal, and to Peter it seemed like a dream come true. Just a few months ago, Peter and Diedrich had sold the **ALLSTAR COMPANY**. Now they were back in business. Together he and Diedrich owned the controlling interest in **DOUGLAS MANUFACTURING**; a new manufacturing company that had a bright future and great growth potential.

The first order of business for Peter, was finding a new location for the company. In the village where **DOUGLAS MANUFACTURING** had started, they operated out of little more than a glorified car garage. Peter knew that as sales increased, they would need more space. The company would also need better and newer equipment as well as more employees.

DOUGLAS MANUFACTURING was looking for a new home and Winkler, Manitoba was the obvious location. It didn't take long for Peter to find the right property. Here they would have room to grow with plenty of space to display their equipment. It was an ideal spot for their new business.

Douglas Manufacturing's annual sales had never reached a hundred thousand dollars. Now with new partners and added operating capital, their first year sales were pushing a half million dollars and the financial bottom line showed a healthy profit.

Selling big ticket items to dealers generally cannot be done by direct mail or telephone only; it usually requires a personal visit from a company representative. This is where Peter Thiessen shines. His confidence and optimism are contagious. While Peter did not enjoy being away from his family, he liked the cash his sales trips generated.

1988 had been a great year for **Douglas.** The sales volume had continued to climb from a half million dollars in 1987, to three million in 1988. Again, the company showed a good profit. Peter could envision the company doing $10 million in sales in 1989.

"This could be a banner year in business for **Douglas Manufacturing,**" Peter thought. He had calculated that if they could increase production to **50 Roto Cutters** per day, they could produce enough products to reach that staggering $10 million projection. As he headed west on his next sales calls, Peter felt good about the future.

The **Douglas Brand** had been on the market now for three years. The company had an above average customer satisfaction rating and the dealers were enjoying strong sales. But as anyone with business experience will tell you, "While growth is good, you can also grow too fast." One of the first indicators is a shortage of cash flow.

Vendors want to be paid on time, and without exception the payroll has to be met. Then there are employee withholdings; they too have to be deposited on time. Peter could tell that the company was getting tight on cash. He was also aware that both he and Diedrich had no more funds to invest. They would need outside capital to fund their growth.

Still, in Peter's mind, a shortage of money did not stop him. He knew there was lots of money available, only this time he didn't have it, but he believed he could get it. During a sales call to an equipment dealer in the province of Saskatchewan, Peter met another businessman who needed a large piece of custom equipment manufactured.

He had a proposal for Peter that would give **Douglas** an advance of $250,000. Peter questioned the man's credibility, but he needed the money so he was willing to pursue the offer. Before heading home to Winkler for the weekend, they agreed to meet again. On Peter's next trip west they would finalize the business arrangement and he would give Peter the advance payment.

Getting back to Winkler, Peter headed straight home where his wife Sara and their four kids and a new baby were waiting for him. It was good to see them again and they were happy to see him. "Sara, you don't need to cook tonight," Peter said. "Kids, get into the car; we are going out to eat." Sara knew it was Peter's way of letting them know he had missed them.

Before leaving town on Monday, Peter met with Diedrich and the other employees at **Douglas Manufacturing**. On the surface everything seemed to be going well, but Peter felt uneasy. He decided to ask a few questions. "Diedrich, about how many **Roto Cutters** are we putting out each day?" He asked. " May be twenty five," was his response.

"How many did you average last week?" Peter wanted to know. "Nineteen per day, was his reply" That was all Peter needed to hear. He knew that the employee morale at the plant was down.

When they had added the new equipment and hired more people their target was to produce 50 **Roto Cutters** per day. Even with added employees, they were producing less than half of their manufacturing projections.

Something had to change and it needed to happen immediately. This was not a one man show. He was getting ready to leave on another sales trip and bring in more orders. He let Diedrich and the other employees know he expected them to meet their quota or face the consequences.

Before leaving town, Peter stopped at a local coffee shop for a quick bite to eat. Philipp Ens, CEO of **TRIPLE E CANADA,** came over to say hello to Peter. Although he and Philipp had met on several occasions, they were only casual acquaintances, but this coffee shop meeting turned out to be a very important event.

Philipp Ens, one of the founding partners in **TRIPLE E CANADA,** was a seasoned businessman. **TRIPLE E** was also the largest Motor Home Manufacturer in Canada. **LODE KING,** the company that had purchased **ALLSTAR** just two years earlier, was a subsidiary of **TRIPLE E. CANADA.**

In the course of their conversation, Philipp asked Peter about **DOUGLAS MANUFACTURING** and how things were going. Not one to keep a lot of secrets, Peter began to tell him about his shortage of capital as well as the man in Saskatchewan who wanted to give him an order, with an advance of $250,000.

"Don't do it!" was Phil's quick response. "I'll let you have the $250,000 right now." Within just hours, Peter had a check in hand from Philipp Ens; but that was just the beginning. There was something about Peter that Phil liked. And there was something about business that Peter needed to learn. Philipp became a mentor to Peter.

Trade shows, trips to see dealers, new distributors in the United States; it seemed wherever Peter went, he came back with more orders. 1989 was going to be a great year for **DOUGLAS MANUFACTURING** and sales should exceed the $10 million mark. The company was out performing its own wild growth projections.

Philipp Ens looked at the financial statements and the growth in sales. As the CEO of **TRIPLE E. CANADA,** he understood the manufacturing business and knew **DOUGLAS MANUFACTURING** was doing well. So well in fact, that he agreed to co-sign a note for an additional $500,000 line of credit that the company needed to fund its growth.

But everything changed on June 12, 1989. The smoke alarms were screaming and the fire alarms were ringing. Soon the **Winkler Volunteer Fire Brigade** trucks were racing down the street. **Douglas Manufacturing** was on fire. Smoke was billowing from the windows as the paint thinners and other flammable items burst into an open flame.

Six hours later it was all over. **Douglas Manufacturing** was in ruins. The building had burned to the ground. What had taken three years to build, had been destroyed by this devastating fire, within just a few hours.

On the bright side; Peter knew **Douglas Manufacturing** was well insured. When you borrow money from the bank or have a bank line of credit, the bank makes sure you have adequate insurance to cover their potential loses.

Still, there were millions of dollars of orders that would not be filled as well as some deposits that would need to be returned. As Peter looked at the charred mess of what used to be **Douglas Manufacturing,** he was sad, but there was one thing that made him happy. There had been no one in the building when it burned, so there was no loss of life and he was thankful for that.

When the fire was reported to the insurance company they were cordial; "We will have our claims adjusters there in a couple of days." The adjusters arrived and with them came a team of investigators. "Before we can pay out the claim, we need to first find the cause of the fire," was their explanation.

That was fine with Peter, or so he thought. But he would soon discover, they didn't just want to find the cause of the fire; the insurance company was trying to get out of paying the claim. Six more weeks and the investigators had a report ready. "The fire had been caused by arson."

The insurance investigation team had determined that somebody had deliberately set the building on fire. Peter's head was spinning. "God, how could this have happened to us?" he wondered. He had a wife and five children that needed his care and financial provision.

Without the money from the insurance company, Peter knew he could not rebuild **DOUGLAS MANUFACTURING**. He decided to call his friend Philipp Ens. He was sure that Phil had already heard about the fire. Everybody in Winkler was talking about it and Peter was sure Phil would have some tough questions for him.

DOUGLAS MANUFACTURING still had a line of credit at the bank and owed almost three quarters of a million dollars. Philipp Ens had his name on the line and Peter was certain the bank would now ask Philipp Ens to pay it.

Peter knew he could not avoid discussing this dreadful situation and decided to face it head on. Sometimes Peter can be brutally blunt and this was one of those times. "Philipp, would you be willing to purchase the remaining assets of **DOUGLAS MANUFACTURING?**" he asked.

"We have good name recognition and a good reputation, with lots of orders and finished products. Also, I believe the cause of the fire will be discovered and the insurance company will have to settle with **DOUGLAS MANUFACTURING.**"

Philipp knew his options were limited. He could negotiate a purchase price with Peter, or risk losing almost a million dollars that was owed to the bank, with the signature of Philipp Ens on bottom line of the note.

"How much would it take," he wanted to know? Peter said, "Give us $50,000 for our equity in **DOUGLAS MANUFACTURING** and it's yours. Write a check of twenty thousand dollars to both me and my partner Dietrich and another ten thousand dollars to Bill Rempel and you own it."

It was a deal. Philipp Ens became the new owner of DOUGLAS MANUFACTURING and what was left of it. Phil was an experienced businessman. This was not what he had expected when he signed the bank note for DOUGLAS MANUFACTURING. But it also was not the end of the story.

It had been nine years since Peter and Sara and their family moved back to Winkler from Mexico. During that time they had owned several homes and started three different businesses. They had lost money; they had made money and even endured a fire.

Sarah, their baby girl had been born during that time and their other children were all attending Canadian public schools and learning to read and speak English.

Winkler had been good to Peter and Sara, but there had also been some bad experiences. Something was stirring in Peter's heart. To make another new beginning in business, maybe they should move to a new location.

Once again it was decision time. Should they go back to Mexico? Peter knew that going back to Mexico would be very difficult for the children and their education. Also, he and Sara had adapted to the less conservative ways of the Mennonites living in Manitoba. He knew of other Mennonite communities in Southern Saskatchewan; would that be a good place to settle?

There was one other location that interested him. It was near Paris, Texas. On one of his recent trips to Mexico, Peter had heard of several Mennonite families from Mexico who had moved and settled in Paris, Texas in recent years. There was lots of land available at reasonable prices in the Paris area. It seemed like a good place to at least consider.

"Sara and the kids might enjoy Texas," he thought to himself. Also, if he started another business, he would have the entire United States as his market. Peter was convinced, or maybe he was trying to convince himself, that Texas was worth investigating.

Again, somewhat reluctantly, Sara agreed; she was willing to pack up the kids and get ready to move. After all she had promised "for better or for worse," she would stay with her husband, Peter. They would sell their home and all their personal belongings and head south for Texas.

Ten years in Winkler, Peter and Sara had accumulated a lot of things. They knew that much of what they had, they would need again, wherever the Thiessen family would decide to settle. "We'll buy a **U-Haul Moving Van**," was Peter's comment. That way they could take some of the more valuable pieces of furniture and other possessions with them to their next location, wherever that was going to be.

When Peter and Sara listed their house for sale, it sold quickly. The equity in their house and the twenty thousand dollars from the sale of **Douglas Manufacturing** totaled just under two hundred thousand dollars. That was about what they had, ten years earlier when they came to Winkler, Manitoba from Mexico,

Peter and Sara Thiessen, now with five children, once again were packed; and on the move, ready to make another new beginning. He may not have known it at the time, but Texas was made for Peter. Everything is big in Texas and Peter liked big things; especially big ideas!

Note:

In 1989 the cause of the fire was determined to have come from a short circuit in an electrical outlet in the building.

Subsequently the insurance company paid for the cost of rebuilding the **Douglas Manufacturing** factory, as well as the equipment and the inventory inside the factory before the fire.

After rebuilding the factory it was put back into operation by Philipp Ens and his management team.

Welcome to Texas
Putting Tigertown on the Map

A s Peter and Sara Thiessen left Winkler Manitoba, they knew they were saying good-bye for the last time. Most likely they would come back for a visit, but it would not be their home again. Heading south on Provincial highway #32 soon they could see the Canada Customs buildings and just to the south was the US Immigration.

As Peter pulled to a stop at the US border, following close behind in the pickup truck, was his wife Sara and their younger children, Frank and little Sarah. The older sons, Peter and Jake were riding with their dad in the cab of the large **U-HAUL MOVING VAN.**

The US Customs Immigration Officer greeted Peter. "Where are you going today?" he wanted to know. "Heading for Texas," was Peter's response. Peter had his passport and the necessary E2 visa ready and gave it to the Officer. "What's in the van," he asked. "Personal belongings and household goods;" Peter's answer seemed to satisfy him as he waved them through and wished them a safe trip.

That was long before 9/11, the fateful day when the TWIN TOWERS IN NEW YORK CITY were destroyed. Since that time, homeland security has made clearing United States customs much more difficult. Now, even the good neighbors from Canada need to have a passport to enter the USA.

Peter had been born in Mexico, but he also had Canadian citizenship papers. Now with an E2 business visa, he felt like a real international businessman. Sara and two of the boys were also born in Mexico, but had become Canadian citizens. The girls in the Thiessen family had both been born in Canada. Without planning, they had become an international family.

Fifteen hundred miles was a long trip for the little caravan that was heading south on US Interstate 29 toward Kansas City, Missouri. Little Sarah enjoyed looking for the next McDONALD's sign. It was always good for a potty break, and if they hit it right, maybe they would get a hamburger with fries and a soft ice cream cone for dessert.

The Thiessen family was a hardy bunch and sleeping in the truck and van was nothing unusual. In Peter's opinion, enduring a little bit of hardship is good for anyone. "That's why truck stops and restaurants have rest-rooms," Peter explained to the kids. "When you drive all night, in the morning you can have breakfast."

The second day on the road, they were in new territory. On other trips to Mexico, by now they would be heading west. But this time they were heading south of Kansas City on State highway 71, toward Interstate 44. Turning right on I-44, soon the sign said, "Tulsa 100 miles."

Peter didn't know it, but Tulsa, Oklahoma would become an important location in his business future.

Peter himself would deliver truckloads of **PJ TRAILERS** to equipment dealers in Tulsa. Still later, he and Sara as well as other members in their family would establish close relationships with new friends in Tulsa, Oklahoma.

Just past the Arkansas River in Tulsa, Oklahoma is the I-44 and highway 75 junction. Heading south on State highway 75; they were on the home stretch. Soon they would pass the City of McAlester, a maximum security prison.

Here is where some of America's meanest prisoners were locked up. Oklahoma has been called "Indian Territory" and they were traveling south on the Indian Nations Turnpike. As they exited the toll road, there was a highway road sign that read, "Paris, Texas 62 Miles." In just a few more minutes Peter and his family would be in the big state of Texas.

As they approached Paris, Texas, it was time to take a break. Paris was not a big city like Winnipeg Manitoba, Kansas City, or even Tulsa, Oklahoma. But compared to Winkler it did seem rather large. Driving south on Texas state highway 271, they could see the large **CAMPBELL SOUP** sign.

The **CAMPBELL SOUP COMPANY** has been and still is one of the main employers in Paris, Texas. In the southwest corner of the city of Paris is the other major employer in the area. It is **KIMBERLY CLARK KLEENEX COMPANY.**

With a population of just over 25,000, the residents of Paris are pleased to have two nationally recognized companies in their city.

Peter and Sara Thiessen had arrived in Paris, but where was Tigertown? With a name like that, the kids may have been looking for the zoo. No, Tigertown did not have caged animals. It was a place where people really lived and they would soon be there.

Three Mennonite families from Mexico had moved to Tigertown, Texas in recent years. Peter had their names and phone numbers. He also had the directions that would take them to Tigertown. After a quick bite to eat, the small Thiessen caravan headed out on the final phase of their trip. Their last destination was Tigertown, twenty miles west of Paris.

In less than thirty minutes on the road they could see the sign that read "Tigertown." There was no Post Office and no railroad station. The town had no churches and no library. There was just one small convenience store with a couple of gas pumps. Suddenly Winkler looked like a metropolis!

Tigertown didn't know it yet, but there was going to be a population explosion. Peter and Sara Thiessen and their five children had come to town. They had come to make a new beginning in a new place. One day he would be responsible for hundreds of people moving from various other Mennonite communities and relocating to Tigertown, Texas.

Providing a house for Sara and their family was always a top priority for Peter. There were numerous houses available, but more than just a house, Peter wanted one that came with a sizeable property. He spotted a for sale sign at 1779 FM Rd #2352. It was a three bedroom house on a five acre lot.

Sara knew that this house was not as nice as the one they had in Winkler, but since they were making a new beginning, this would be a good place to start. Peter had come with cash in hand and this property seemed priced right. He made an offer and the seller accepted it. This was the first piece of real estate they owned as residents of Texas.

Soon the **U-Haul Van** was unloaded and the furniture moved into place. Now it was time for Sara to set up the house the way she wanted it to be. There was a master bedroom and it even had its own bathroom.

Lisa, a teenager by now, needed her own room. The three boys could certainly share a room and little Sarah would have to sleep in her own bed in Lisa's room.

Never one to procrastinate, Peter knew he would need immediate income. But he was not looking for a job; he was looking for a business opportunity. What could he manufacture that he could also market? He had lots of ideas.

It wasn't long before Peter had a 40' by 60' shop erected on the vacant property behind the house they just bought. He didn't know it at the time, but within six months it would become the home of **PJ Trailers.**

Although building a business was important to Peter, his top priority was providing for his family. He knew what he would do; he had done it before. He would buy used farm equipment and export it to Mexico.

Running on Empty
Hearing God's Voice at the Filling Station

Wherever Peter went with his pickup truck, he was likely pulling a trailer. Being in the used farm equipment business, he never knew when or where he would find the next piece of farm equipment he might want to buy.

A plow or a cultivator; a planter; even a small tractor would fit on the trailer and save him from having to make another trip to pick it up. That day Peter had made a purchase from a local farm implement dealer and was headed for home.

He noticed the gas gauge on his truck was running low and he decided to stop at a neighborhood service station to fill up the truck. A rather curious older man owned the gas station and came over to the truck where Peter was pumping gas. Looking at Peter's pickup truck and trailer he asked, "Where did you get that trailer?"

"I bought it," was Peter's blunt reply.

"You should be building trailers," the old guy continued. "As a matter of fact, there is a young man not far from here, who had a small trailer factory and he recently went bankrupt. You should go and see him. Likely you can buy what he has left over, real cheap."

As strange as it seemed, suddenly what he had heard, perked Peter's interest. He asked for the young man's name. Peter began thinking, "It might be a good idea to pay a visit to the closed trailer factory." Peter made a mental note; the guy's name was Robert Fults. Before heading for home, he also got Robert's phone number.

It was only a day or so, before Peter Thiessen gave Robert Fults a call. He asked Robert if he could come to see the bankrupt trailer factory. "You don't want to see it," Robert said. "It's all junk If you want to build trailers, hire me and I will show you how to do it."

Robert's blunt offer caught Peter by surprise. As they continued the phone call, what Peter discovered was amazing. Robert Fults had started building trailers when he was just a kid, sixteen years of age. No doubt, Robert was an unusual young man with engineering and manufacturing skills.

Peter could see that Robert had also done remarkably well in sales. In just two short years, Robert already had over twenty dealers who had been selling his trailers. "Let me discuss this with my family" were Peter's final words. "I will call you back soon."

Peter discovered that something had gone wrong in Robert's life; he could understand it from his own experience. Like Peter, Robert had started drinking at a young age. It was alcohol that had become Robert's downfall. This was a big problem to Peter. He had young sons and he did not want them exposed to the evils of alcohol.

Robert remained on Peter's mind and he had to call him back. It was the next day when Peter finally made the call. "I'm calling about your offer to help us build a trailer factory," Peter began. Robert responded quickly. "Hire me and I will show you how to build trailers. I can also introduce you to the dealers who will buy them. They will sell all the trailers you can build." Robert was definitely getting Peter's attention.

There had been times in his life, when Peter knew God was speaking to him. "Was this another one of those times?" he wondered. Peter liked Robert and what he had to offer. He seemed to have a positive outlook on life and Peter liked that too. But there was one thing that really bothered Peter; it was Robert's problem with alcohol.

"Robert," Peter said, "I am willing to give you a job and I will pay you well. But you told me that you had a drinking problem and for that reason I cannot hire you to work for me."

"What can I do to change your mind," asked Robert. "Quit drinking," Peter replied. "If I hire you, as long as you work for me, you cannot take a drink."

It seemed like Robert had been looking for someone who would hold him accountable. Without any hesitation he said, "It's a deal! When do we start the new trailer business?" "Now," was Peter's quick reply.

As Peter and Robert finished a very important phone call, they both knew something good was going to come out of this new venture. The new warehouse Peter built behind their house would become the new trailer factory.

Never one to complicate things, Peter decided to call the new business, **PJ TRAILERS**. Those were the initials of his oldest two sons, Peter and Jake. He knew they would be working in the new trailer factory so **PJ TRAILERS** seemed like a good name for the new company.

Now it was time to go shopping. Peter and Robert were heading for Lubbock, Texas. Peter knew much of what they needed for their new trailer manufacturing business. Building trailers would be quite similar to what they had done at **COMSTAR, ALLSTAR** and **DOUGLAS MANUFACTURING** in Winkler.

Still, some things were new to him but he was willing to learn from his young new associate. Robert had good contacts in the manufacturing business in Lubbock and that is where they were headed. They would need welders and electric saws, as well as lots of hand tools like drills and electric sanders.

Tigertown to Lubbock, Texas was 400 miles; about an eight hour drive. They had lots of time to talk and time passed quickly. Normally Peter is the one who does a lot of the talking. This time he was the student and willing to listen and learn. Robert had the experience, so he became the teacher. Peter may have been limited in his use of the English language, but he has a mind that is able to remember what he hears.

They came from very opposite backgrounds, but they still had a lot in common. Robert came from a well-to-do home in Paris, Texas. His father had a good position with **CAMPBELL SOUP**. Peter, on the other hand had been born into a very modest home in a Mennonite Village in Mexico.

They both had an entrepreneurial spirit and enjoyed business ventures at an early age. The other thing was, they both had been tempted and yielded to the lure of alcohol. By the help of God, Peter had overcome what he called "Being a drunk." He cared about his young friend Robert and wanted to help him if he could. Peter knew it was Robert's decision.

After spending twenty thousand dollars, their pickup truck was loaded with everything that Peter and Robert would need to begin **PJ TRAILER MANUFACTURING**. Axles, wheels, tires, running lights and hitches would be shipped later. Now it was time to get down to business.

Peter Thiessen and his sons, Peter Jr. and Jake were the first employees of the new company, **PJ TRAILER MANUFACTURING,** located in Tigertown, Texas. Robert Fults was the unofficial shop foreman. Setting up all the tools and other equipment they had purchased in Lubbock was exciting. Peter felt right at home in this environment. Once again he was in business for himself.

The first order of business was getting the welders hooked up. Peter knew from his years of manufacturing in Winkler, that welders require a lot of electricity.

The needed rewiring and additional industrial outlets were quickly installed. Now it was time to get the manufacturing started. Watching the flash of the arc welders added to the excitement of this new project.

Summer days in Texas can be hot so the "air conditioning" needed to be turned on. At **PJ TRAILERS,** that meant opening the doors on both sides and adding a large fan to keep the air moving. Summer days in Winkler had been more enjoyable, but then, winter was coming and it would be much more enjoyable in Texas during those months.

Today every modern trailer factory needs to have a paint booth, where the finished trailers are painted. The first **PJ TRAILERS** paint booth was under the open sky of Tigertown. When conditions were right, the wind was calm and the bugs still asleep, the **PJ TRAILERS** painting crew applied the final touches to the finished product.

It had only been a couple of weeks and already the first **PJ TRAILERS** were coming off this four man assembly line. To Peter those first units looked like a work of art. Here was a new product that had his new **PJ TRAILER** decals on it.

Robert had promised that the buyers would be ready and now it was time to make the first sales calls and get the business sales revenue coming in.

PJ Trailers, Inc.
The Beginning of Something Big

R obert was right. He had given Peter a list of recommended equipment dealers who would buy their new trailers. After just a few phone calls the trailers were all sold. While the rest of the company's trailer assembly line kept on working, Peter got to make the deliveries.

He enjoyed that part of the business. It gave him the opportunity to meet the dealers and get information on what they liked and didn't like about his trailers. More than anything else, Peter wanted **PJ TRAILER** buyers to be satisfied customers. If there was a problem, he wanted to be the first to know about it.

Soon trailers were stacked on trailers and hitched to a pickup truck. Peter was on his way to make his first deliveries. In those early **PJ TRAILER** days, it wasn't uncommon to drive down the highway and see what looked like an abandoned **PJ TRAILER** sitting in the ditch

Here is what sometimes happened. Bouncing along the road, the retaining chains on the top trailer had begun to slip. Without the driver even knowing it, the trailer had come loose. The swaying of the load caused the loose trailer to flip and roll off the highway.

Without any fanfare, soon another one of **PJ Trailers** pickup trucks was headed out to retrieve the abandoned trailer. This was not a frequent occurrence, but it happened more times than Peter likes to recall. Looking back on the incidents; the liability exposure this created could have been horrendous and costly.

To Peter this was simply a trailer endurance test. Now he could say that **PJ Trailers** were made to withstand a high speed impact without a broken weld or other major damage. A bit of paint touch-up and it would be ready for delivery on the next load. Peter reminded the loading crew, "Make sure that the next load of trailers is well tied down."

After just six months of business, **PJ Trailers** needed more manufacturing space. It was time to grow and expand. Peter decided to add a new 100' by 200' wing to the existing building. In addition to more manufacturing space,

PJ Trailers also needed to build larger inside paint booths Painting trailers in the outside open air was working fine. The quality of the paint jobs was acceptable and without customer complaints. It was the neighbors who were complaining. The odor of paint over-spray was drifting in the wind and carried over into nearby residential areas.

When **OSHA** came by to inspect the **PJ Trailers** operation, they wanted to see the paint booth. Looking at the outside location, there was paint on the grass. Environmentally this was not acceptable. If **PJ Trailers** wanted to continue, they would need to do their painting inside in paint booths that met all the necessary **OSHA** requirements.

As the first year of business came to a close, Peter felt good about what they had been able to accomplish. **PJ Trailers** had built and sold more than three thousand trailers. Company sales were approaching a half million dollars and there were more than 20 people on the payroll.

Looking back to when he first met Robert, Peter knew there would be those who would say it was good luck. To Peter it was "good," but not luck. It was a divine appointment. Every morning and evening he was praying for wisdom and the blessing of God on **PJ Trailers** and its employees. There was no doubt in Peter's heart; "When we pray in faith, God hears and answers our prayers."

As the New Year arrived, it was also time to set new goals. "We built three thousand trailers last year. This year, let's make it six thousand," was Peter's bold announcement to his employees. "We only built single axle units," he continued, "but from now on, we are going to also build tandem axles and goose neck trailers."

Peter was a man of his word. His various parts suppliers trusted **PJ Trailers** and gave them extended terms. Some were willing to go ninety days before asking for payment. This helped a lot but even then, there were times when it was hard to meet payroll. Peter knew he needed to have a business bank that was willing to work with him in his growing business.

He was a Canadian with an E2 visa, who had moved to Texas within the last two years. **PJ Trailers** was a relatively new business without a track record. It was not easy to find a bank that would extend a line of credit to someone with such limited business credentials.

Peter Thiessen had brought a document from Canada that he valued. It was a letter of recommendation from Philipp Ens, one of the founders of **Triple E Canada. He** had written it on Peter's behalf before he and his family had moved to Texas.

Peter began to visit local banks in Paris, Texas. The letter from Phil Ens made Peter feel good about himself. If Phil believed in him, and Peter believed in himself, surely somewhere there would be a banker who would also believe in him and want his business.

Persistence paid off. It wasn't long until Peter had a line of credit of one hundred thousand dollars for **PJ Trailers** established at a commercial bank in Paris, Texas. Life was good; **PJ Trailers** was doing well and Peter and Sara's kids were getting more involved. It really was a growing family business.

Being a family business, it was also common to bring food to the business and for the family to eat together. One unforgettable day Jake Thiessen, the second son, quiet by nature, was eating a steak sandwich. Standing alone, almost unnoticed by the others, he started to collapse.

It was obvious that he had swallowed something and he was choking. Not trained in **CPR,** other than slapping his back, none of the other family members knew what to do. Lisa, Jake's older sister remembered that Shari Slaughter, one of the office employees had taken recent **CPR** classes.

Lisa rushed back to the adjacent factory building and asked Shari to come and help. This was serious and there was no time to be lost. Quickly Shari rushed to his aid and began to administer **CPR** to Jake but it seemed as though it was too late. Jake's body seemed lifeless and his lips were turning blue.

Paris, Texas was twenty miles away, but still someone called "911" asking for emergency medical assistance. Not one to give up, Shari applied **CPR** one more time. This time something popped and Jake was able to breathe again. It was only minutes, but it seemed liked hours, until Jake's breathing became normal.

More than an office employee; more than entering sales data or running reports, Shari Slaughter was a caring individual. Jake thought that maybe she was an angel.

Shortly after this serious incident, Shari approached Jake and asked him a very serious question. "If you had not revived, where would you have spent eternity?" She wanted to know.

Jake Thiessen is quiet and contemplative. At the moment he seemed unsure and was not ready to give her an answer. For a moment there was an awkward silence. Shari was not trying to be pushy or to embarrass Jake with her question. She was genuinely concerned about him as a friend and fellow employee.

There came a day when Jake Thiessen was ready to make the greatest decision he would ever make. In his own quiet way, Jake prayed to receive Jesus as his Savior.

Forged Business Cards

Be Sure Your Sin Will Find You Out

Robert Fults, the young man who introduced Peter Thiessen to the trailer manufacturing industry had always given Peter good information. He knew where to get the best trailer building equipment and who were the better trailer parts suppliers. He even had a good list of equipment dealers to contact.

But there was one piece of information that he gave Peter that did not turn out so good. It was a trailer broker contact that Robert had referred. Supposedly he was a distributor who sold trailers to equipment dealers. According to Robert, he was the right person to help build a dealer network.

Peter and Sara were on their way to a funeral in Ontario, Canada. Speeding down the highway in Missouri, they passed an equipment dealer's lot. There Peter spotted some **PJ TRAILERS.** This was an opportunity he could not pass up.

Peter enjoyed walking into a dealer's office for a surprise visit, never knowing what he might learn. This was a visit where the surprise would be on him. "I'm with PJ Trailers," he told the receptionist. "Is the boss available?"

Peter didn't know it, but the boss was in his office and had a machine gun on his lap. On the floor were hundreds of rounds of ammunition. He was waiting for the PJ Trailers guy to show up. He had a score he wanted to settle with him and he was ready.

As Peter would soon find out, there was someone who was posing as the new owner of PJ Trailers. He had been buying PJ Trailers and reselling them to other equipment dealers under false pretenses.

To protect both the innocent and maybe the guilty, we will call him Mr. June. He had been setting up equipment dealers in Missouri to sell PJ Trailers, telling them that he, Mr. June, was the owner of the company. To validate his claim, he had taken Peter Thiessen's business card and crossed off Peter's name and replaced it with his own.

His reason; he told dealers that he, (Mr. June) had just bought PJ Trailers and at the moment was still using Peter's business cards as his own. On the surface this may have seemed innocent but it certainly was foolish. Here was the rest of the story.

As the supposed new owner of PJ Trailers, he had offered extremely generous terms to the trailer dealers. "Buy my trailers," he said, "and if you have not sold them within ninety days, I will take them back and pay 20% interest on each unsold trailer."

To sweeten the deal, he offered "his dealers" an exclusive territory. "Become my dealer and there will not be another PJ Trailer dealer within fifty miles," he promised. There was only one catch to his generosity; all orders had to be paid in cash.

The trailer dealers in any given area know each other. It wasn't long before the Missouri dealers discovered that their "fifty mile exclusive territories" overlapped. Some dealers were within fifteen miles of each other.

Week after week Mr. June had been picking up inventory from **PJ Trailers.** His check was always good for the previous week's pickup and his order volume was on the increase. But his "generous offer" obviously only worked with new dealers.

Peter discovered that the dealer he was visiting had left message after message for Mr. June. He had trailers that had not sold and needed to be picked up. The messages ended with, "Please bring the 20% check for the money we tied up in the trailer purchase."

Mr. June may have ignored the message this dealer had left, but now the real owner of **PJ Trailers** was inside the dealership and it was time to settle the score. As Peter walked into the dealership office, he did not know what to expect.

"You're not the owner," the dealer said. "Mr. June is the man I want to see. He made fancy promises to us about having exclusive territories; he also promised me a 20% return on unsold trailers; he took my check and he cashed it; Mr. June is who I want to see."

"Be thankful you are not him," he continued. Pointing to the machine gun and the pile of ammunition, he said, "These bullets were meant for him." Peter knew the guy was serious and at the moment, did not know what to say.

"Let me assure you," Peter began, "I am the real owner of **PJ Trailers.** My family and I started the business. It is our Company and we never sold it to Mr. June. How can we cleanup this crazy mess." he asked? Peter knew the guy believed him. Now the ball was in the dealer's court.

"Tell me where I can find June," he insisted. "When I find him I will kill him." It almost seemed funny, but Peter did not want to be an accomplice to murder, even though Mr. June had obviously acted very foolishly. Peter promised to do his best to have June call back the dealer.

Peter had an idea; with Mr. June out of the way, he could offer better discounts on **PJ Trailers.** They could also trade out the trailer inventory the dealer had that was not selling. By the time Peter was ready to head north to Canada, he knew he had made a friend out of an enemy.

As Peter and Sara left the lot, the dealer reminded Peter, "Tell June to call me; if he doesn't I am going to get him." Peter wondered how this could be resolved. He knew what Mr. June had done was stupid. Still, he didn't want to see him dead. This guy was mad and Peter took his threats seriously.

When Peter and Sara got back from Canada he knew he had to deal with Mr. June. June would be bringing a check shortly, and wanting to pick up another load of trailers. That would give him the opportunity to confront him. It was only a matter of days until June showed up.

Peter Thiessen can be blunt; and this meeting demanded bluntness. "Mr. June," Peter said, "you need to call the dealers you set up in Missouri and tell them the truth. You do not own **PJ Trailers.** You gave them territories that don't exist. You offered them interest on unsold trailers that you cannot pay. It's time to get on the phone. Do it now."

Peter handed him the phone and turned on the speaker. "Here is the first one to call," he insisted. It was the angry dealer Peter had just met. "This is Mr. June," he began. "I am calling to let you know I am coming to pick up the trailers you have not sold."

As the phone call ended, Peter knew that his relationship with Mr. June was over. Although June had moved a lot of trailers, Peter knew the reputation of **PJ Trailers** was much more important than short term sales volume. "Mr. June," Peter said, "our relationship is over."

It was only a matter of a few days until Mr. June returned to **PJ Trailers.** This time he had his wife with him. Sitting in Peter's office, June was in tears. "If I lose my job, my wife will divorce me," he said. "She works at the bank and has helped cover my checks to **PJ TRAILERS,**" he continued.

Mr. June was trying every trick in the book, to get Peter to change his mind, but Peter stood firm. "Have you picked up the unsold trailers," Peter wanted to know. "If I were you, I would do that as soon as possible. It could be good for your own health."

What Mr. June did not know; the dealer in Missouri had cooled down a little. Murder was no longer on his mind. However he had talked to the local police chief in the small Missouri town. If Mr. June came to town, the dealer and his sons had agreed they would give him a whipping, while local law enforcement agreed to look the other way.

Although Peter was unhappy with what June had done, he still did not want to see him get hurt. Again he reminded Mr. June, "For your own good, go and pick up the trailers and make things right with the Missouri dealers you set up."

The episode also taught Peter a lesson. He knew Robert had referred Mr. June with good intentions. Looking back, he could see that Robert had been immature in making the referral, and Peter had been reckless in allowing someone to represent **PJ TRAILERS,** without doing a proper background check on Mr. June.

Peter, God and the Banker

Learning to do Business God's Way

Twenty million dollars is a lot of sales volume for a little company. That is where **PJ TRAILERS** was in 1996. In spite of being profitable as a business, the company was still struggling financially and Peter was tired of it. He needed more operating capital and had tried to get it, but he couldn't seem to find a bank willing to help him anywhere.

He had been able to get extended terms from his suppliers, but even that had its limits. Peter was aware that if he could purchase larger quantities of steel, axles, wheels and tires and pay cash, he would get much better discounts and that would affect the bottom line dramatically.

The letter of recommendation he had received from Philipp Ens, the CEO of **TRIPLE E CANADA,** had helped him get an initial hundred thousand dollar bank line of credit, but that is where it had stopped. At one point Peter had even offered to pledge the 45 land titles he had to the "manufactured housing development," to the bank, but to no avail.

Call it pride or ignorance, there was a secret Peter had not been willing to share with bankers, lawyers and accountants; he could not read or write in the English language. In Mexico where he had been born, Mennonites placed little or no value on education, and he got little of it.

In the past, it seemed that all he had needed to do business was a pocket calculator, but not anymore. Perhaps it was a self imposed limitation; but Peter had reached the breaking point. He was weary of trying to do things his own way.

He enjoyed business, but from now on, he wanted to "do business God's way." That was Peter's attitude, late that afternoon, when he locked the door on his office. His wife Sara knew how serious he was.

Together they had lived through a lot. They had seen the good and the bad in life. Selling a business and making a good profit and then losing everything in a fire; they had experienced it all.

It wasn't that Peter was in a "giving up" frame of mind. Rather, he wanted to "give over" his business to God. Although he had been raised in an ultraconservative, Old Colony Church, he had come to understand the grace of God. Peter knew it was not his own goodness, but rather the goodness of God that had brought him into a personal relationship with his heavenly father.

As he began to pray, his prayer was not elegant, but it was fervent and effective. Like the prophet Elijah on Mount Carmel, Peter was calling out to God to reveal himself. "Father," he prayed, "I want to give you my business, but I would appreciate it, if you would let me manage it."

"Lord," he continued, "I want to learn how to do business God's way. As my offering, I will give away at least 20% of the profits from my business ventures. And Lord," he concluded, "when I am able to help someone financially, I will tell them it is your money and not mine, that I am giving away."

Peter doesn't remember if he said "Amen" to his prayer, but looking back now, he knows God heard it and he answered him. While he was still sitting there alone in his office, there was a knock at the door. When Peter reluctantly opened the door, he didn't see God or hear his voice. Rather it was someone God had sent. It was the banker from Paris, Texas.

Peter was amazed at the banker's story. Within the past hour, while Peter had been talking to God, God had been talking to the banker. The banker did not know Peter and Peter did not know the banker. However both Peter and the banker knew God, and they both knew his voice.

The warmth Peter felt in his heart that afternoon was not from eating too much Mexican food, nor was it the Texas heat. He knew it was the presence of God. Suddenly Peter knew that he was free to share what he had been hiding for such a long time.

"Mr. Banker," he began, "I want you to know I cannot read or write and that has caused me a lot of problems. When bankers ask me for a business plan, I do not know how to present it." By now the banker was grinning. He knew that this was no ordinary business meeting. He too had heard the voice of God at his bank. Now it was time to do business.

"Peter," he said, "you do the talking and I will do the writing. Show me what you have and what you need and I will put it on paper." For a moment, Peter was speechless.

As Peter, the businessman and Pat, the banker walked through the **PJ TRAILER** facility, life had never looked better or more exciting to either one of them.

Here were two men that God had supernaturally brought together in answer to a simple but sincere prayer. They didn't know it at the time, but this meeting would turn into a long and lasting relationship that both of them would cherish in the future.

"Peter, what do you need?" was the banker's blunt question. "A million dollar line of credit," was Peter's blunt answer. "I will have it for you within 72 hours," was the banker's reply.

It was time for the banker to go back to Paris, Texas and Peter needed to go home and tell Sara about this remarkable experience. As he walked into the house, he tried to contain his joy, but Sara could see it on his face. "What happened?" she wanted to know.

"God has heard our prayer. We have a million dollar line of credit available at a new bank in Paris, Texas," he explained. The past months had been tough for both of them. But now the clouds had lifted and the sun was shining again.

It was time to go celebrate. "You don't need to cook tonight," Peter said. "I am taking you out to dinner. What will it be, Mexican or chicken?" As they were going out to Paris for dinner, they didn't need to have the radio playing. There was a song of thanksgiving in their hearts.

That night as they knelt by their bed, it was easy to pray. All that Peter wanted to say was a big "Thank you" to a loving heavenly Father, who hears and answers prayer.

To Sara it wasn't so much about the money. Seeing the weight Peter had carried in recent months lifted off his shoulders, she too whispered a special "Thank you" to God.

Daddy's Little Girl
Delayed Wedding Plans

When Peter and Sara Thiessen moved to Paris, Texas from Canada, Lisa, the older of their two daughters had remained in Winkler. She was still in high school and wanted to finish her final school year in Canada.

High school graduation was important to Lisa. Because Canadian school standards equaled, and in some respects exceeded US school standards, it made good sense for Lisa to spend her last school year in Winkler, Manitoba.

In addition to getting an education, Lisa had also fallen in love or maybe it was Pete Zacharias who fell in love with Lisa. No matter who fell first, they wanted to be together and had talked seriously about getting married to each other.

The Zacharias family lived in Southern, Manitoba and owned a meat packing business. It was a business Pete knew and enjoyed. He was just now old enough to become a working business partner to his father. But over the past months, he seemed more interested in being with Lisa than in making smoked sausages.

With her family living in Texas, Lisa went south for a visit. It wasn't long after she arrived that her father, Peter Thiessen found a job for her at **PJ TRAILERS.** Both her brothers Peter and Jake were already working in the business. Cutting steel and installing wood trailer flooring kept them busy.

Peter knew that Lisa did not belong in the shop. Up to that time she was the most educated of the five kids in the family and Peter wanted to take advantage of her schooling. It was the early 1990s and already **PJ TRAILERS** was computerized. This would be Lisa's assignment; get the accounting and product inventory set up on the computer.

Lisa enjoyed her new work assignment. It gave her a feeling of worth. Her years in school had been a good investment of time, on her part. Although Peter had a very limited education, he was good with numbers and he liked the quick information that Lisa was able to provide when he asked for it.

In the evening and on weekends, Lisa and Pete Zacharias spent a lot of time on the phone. They were getting serious about marriage and even had a wedding date picked. But it wasn't a good date; at least not to her father.

PJ TRAILERS was still in its infancy and needed Peter's full attention and Peter needed Lisa to help him at the business, so he asked them to change their wedding date. It was not an easy decision, but ultimately Lisa and her fiancé Pete, agreed that it would be alright to move the wedding date by three months.

When the new wedding date finally arrived, Lisa was happy they had waited. Her mother and father had done their best to make it a wedding day their oldest daughter Lisa would long remember. Old friends and family coming from Canada, and new friends from Texas making them welcome; it was an extravaganza event for the entire family

Peter Thiessen has an ability to assess strengths and weakness in people rather quickly. He knew that Lisa had made a good choice in a husband. Pete Zacharias was a motivated young man with leadership ability and Peter Thiessen had a place for him in **PJ Trailers.**

PJ Trailers had offices in both Canada and the United States, so getting an L-1 visa for Pete and Lisa was not difficult. Soon Pete was promoted to general manager at **PJ Trailers** in Texas.

In addition, Pete and Lisa spent many of the summer months in Canada promoting **PJ Canada,** the Canadian division of the **PJ Trailers Company.**

While Pete enjoyed the cooler Canadian summers, there was another hidden benefit that the Canadian operation brought to **PJ Trailers.** Canada had high quality standards for trailers being imported. At the moment, **PJ Trailers** did not meet some of those stringent requirements.

It was at a Regina, Saskatchewan trailer trade show that Pete first became aware of this. When Pete brought his recommended improvements to the table, everyone involved agreed; "Whatever it takes, we will build the best trailers on the market anywhere."

That one very important quality control decision, has helped to make **PJ Trailers** one of the leading trailer manufacturers in the Nation. To this day, the Company has maintained a stellar reputation as an industry leader in North America.

At its peak, before the sale of the company, **PJ Trailers** was building and selling in excess of 45,000 trailers per year. (A trailer every 7 minutes, 24 hours per day, 6 days a week)

PJ Trailers did this with less than 1% of annual revenues spent in advertising. Proof that even in today's high tech world; satisfied customers are still the best source of advertising.

Creating a New Community

Providing Manufactured Homes for Employees

B usiness was booming at **PJ TRAILERS** in Tigertown, Texas. Just a few years ago they had started with just four employees; and that even included Peter Thiessen and his oldest two sons Peter Jr. and Jake. Now there were more than twenty-five people working at the plant.

Each month, as orders increased, so did the need for additional help, and often good help was hard to find. Word soon got out in other Mennonite communities that **PJ TRAILERS,** a manufacturing plant in Tigertown, Texas was hiring welders and other construction workers.

It attracted Mennonites living in other locations in Texas and in the surrounding states. Many of them had been born into an agricultural Mennonite community and grown up in Mexico. Repairing equipment and building barns and houses was part of their everyday life.

More than eighty years had passed since the initial migration from Canada had taken place. The 700 plus families who came in the 1920s had multiplied Mennonite style. There were now as many as 100,000 Mennonites in various locations in Mexico and Central America.

These were changing times and not everyone in the communities had a desire to remain on the farm. In addition, farming in Mexico required substantial capital. From the purchase of land, to farm equipment, as well as irrigation systems; it took hundreds of thousands of dollars to get started. Few young families had that kind of resources.

While there were always jobs available in the farming industry in Mexico, work in other industries was somewhat limited. For that reason many Mennonite families had come to the United States of America and settled in Texas, Oklahoma and Kansas.

Throughout their history, Mennonite people have lived in communities. This happened in Russia, Canada, Mexico and now also in the United States. Still today, the magnet that holds them together is the local church. Generally before a family considers a move, one of the first requirements is the existence of Mennonite churches in the area.

With a reputation of being hard working and intuitive people, finding work usually was not difficult for Mennonite workers. This is especially true in the construction and manufacturing trade. Growing up on the farm had been sort of like a vocational school, where the young learned a useful trade by experience.

It wasn't long before new employees began arriving in Tigertown, Texas. Often they had large families. More than a job, they needed a place to live. Adding new employees created a need for more housing and Tigertown, with a population of under a hundred residents, did not have many vacancies.

Peter decided to start a housing development where these new families could come and live. This seemed like a win/win idea to

Peter. It could meet his labor needs, help families make an above average income and bless people spiritually. Why not? He was willing to give it a try.

Purchasing a sizeable acreage adjacent to the **PJ TRAILERS** plant, he began setting up manufactured homes. Peter made them available for rent to his new employees. Tenants who chose to stay were given a purchase option on their home sites. It was a novel idea that was also very practical.

Now **PJ TRAILERS** had employees living within walking distance of the plant. They were able to live in modern, air-conditioned homes and enjoy modern conveniences. The result; Peter had loyal employees and they had the opportunity to become home owners without making a big investment. And, yes there were Mennonite churches in the area, and more would be built soon.

By the end of the year, there were twenty-five new homes sitting on this new, neat looking housing edition. Once again company sales had doubled. **PJ TRAILERS** had built 12,000 plus trailers in the previous year, and what was important to Peter, the company was showing a profitable bottom line.

Again, Peter had set the high goal of doubling production and sales in the coming year. Building 25,000 trailers in the **PJ TRAILER** factory was a lot of work. It would require even more employees as well as operating capital and that had to come from more sales.

To accommodate the additional workers, Peter expanded the housing development. He purchased more land and created a new subdivision. This time he set it up to accommodate double-wide manufactured homes and made them available on the same lease/option offer.

Again by the end of the year the company had exceeded Peter's high goals and at the same time they had added twenty-eight more homes for the additional new employees. Peter was not planning to be a real estate developer, but at one point, he held the title to forty-five new homes, each sitting on its own developed lot.

Each of these homes needed groceries, clothes, cars and whatever a normal family needs to live. As hard working, well paid employees they had extra money to spend. More than just providing PJ TRAILERS with good workers, it was also good for the economy in the Tigertown area.

In the early 1900s Tigertown, Texas had its own post office, but it closed in 1905. Today it has one convenience store and a local welding shop. There now is a Mennonite church at the edge of town and several more within ten miles of Tigertown.

Currently there are about eight more trailer manufactures in the area. Most, if not all of them started by people who got their training at PJ TRAILERS. There are also numerous other business that have sprung up in the area, to fill the needs of those who have come to Tigertown in recent years.

Helping a Brother Start a Business
The State of Texas, is a Good Place to Grow

A lready several other smaller trailer manufacturing plants
had sprung up in the Tigertown, Texas vicinity. Most of
these "new businesses" had been started by individuals who had
worked at **PJ TRAILERS.**

Some of these "new business owners" had learned the trade
as employees at **PJ TRAILERS** and now had become competitors.
Peter Thiessen wasn't worried.

He knew there was more demand in the trailer industry then
they could fill. There always seemed to be more orders than they
could handle. "What harm can one more trailer manufacturer
do?" was his attitude.

The first **PJ TRAILERS** manufactured had been simple, two
wheel utility type trailers, priced at well under a thousand dollars.
By now they had added tandem wheel, goose neck trailers that ran

as high as ten thousand dollars. "We could even build trailers for transport trucks," Peter thought to himself. Then he had an idea.

He had a brother who still lived in Mexico. Like Peter, he had an aptitude for doing business. It seemed to run in the Thiessen family. Peter and Sara decided to help him and his family move from Mexico to Tigertown, Texas.

The plans they had made, were that after they arrived in Texas and were settled down, together Peter and his brother would build another "**Trailer Manufacturing Company.**"

To outsiders it may have looked like the "**New Company**" would be in direct competition with **PJ Trailers,** but Peter could see beyond that point. According to the proposed plan, after the "**New Company**" was in operation, Peter would be entitled to 50% of the net profits.

By July of 1996 Peter's brother had arrived in Texas and the "**New Company**" was started. The "**New Company**" name was **Load Trail, Inc..** The initial plan was for the Company to manufacture enclosed cargo trailers, and certain other trailer models not built by **PJ Trailers.**

During the startup phase of **Load Trail, Inc.,** there was a constant sharing of employees and other resources between the two companies. **PJ Trailers** also provided much of the technology needed to begin the trailer manufacturing process.

Like **PJ Trailers; Load Trail, Inc.,** also produced high quality trailers and the business took off with new trailer orders coming in rapidly. The original staff consisted of 31 employees, with three, one ton trucks delivering the entire product line of trailers to area trailer dealers.

But it wasn't long until **Load Trail, Inc.,** ran out of operating capital. Because it was a new company and without a track record, Peter's brother could not get the bank line of credit the Company needed for day to day operation.

Peter agreed to use the assets of **PJ TRAILERS**, plus his own personal guarantee to collateralize the needed funding, for **LOAD TRAIL, INC.**. But there was one condition; Peter would now become part owner of **LOAD TRAIL, INC.**

It was an exciting day for **LOAD TRAIL, INC.**, when Peter and his brother signed the bank documents. With the needed line of credit in place, **LOAD TRAIL, INC.**, was in a position to become a major trailer manufacturer.

LOAD TRAIL, INC., had started as a small business in 1996, in a single 50,000 square foot manufacturing facility on 18 acres. In just a few short years the company had grown to approximately 370,000 square feet.

Since the inception of the Company, the staff had grown to over 400 employees. The delivery vehicle count had increased dramatically to over 30 **PETERBILTS, FREIGHTLINERS** and **VOLVO TRACTORS. LOAD TRAIL, INC.** The Company Peter Thiessen and his brother had started, had become a thriving enterprise in the Tigertown, Texas community.

Anyone visiting this industrial area just two miles west of Tigertown will recognize that these two trailer manufacturing giants are important to both the local economy as well as to the state of Texas.

PJ Trailers in Mexico
Back to the Beginning

FORD MOTOR COMPANY was doing it; so were VOLKSWAGEN and NISSAN. Recently WHIRLPOOL and SONY had set up shop here as well. These companies had all opened manufacturing plants in Mexico.

"Why not **PJ TRAILERS**" Peter Thiessen thought to himself. After all this is where he had been born and he wouldn't even need a translator.

With the growth of **PJ TRAILERS** in Tigertown, Texas it made good business sense to set up a manufacturing plant in Cuauhtémoc, Mexico. Since the passage of **NAFTA** (The North American Free Trade Agreement) import/export regulations had made doing business in Mexico much easier and there were even some tax advantages.

On his next trip to Mexico, Peter decided to look into the possibility of setting up a **PJ TRAILERS** manufacturing plant in the same community where he once lived. He knew the people and he understood their culture and spoke their language. The more he thought about setting up a **PJ TRAILER** plant in Mexico, the more he liked the idea.

On `the highway heading north from Cuauhtémoc toward the Mennonite villages, Peter found an eight acre plot of land available at a good price. When the City of Cuauhtémoc was willing to give him the necessary permits to begin construction, to Peter it looked like the light was green.

It was time to set up shop and start building **PJ TRAILERS** in Mexico. Soon the bulldozers began leveling the ground where the manufacturing plant would be built. Modeled after the factory in Tigertown, the building went up fast.

It was good to be able to learn from the successes of the past, but also valuable to avoid making some of the mistakes they had experienced. Many of the workers they were hiring, he had known since he was a kid selling tools in his stand on the streets of Cuauhtémoc.

Within 90 days **PJ TRAILERS** in Mexico was up and running. Peter had been there during most of the building phase. He had acted as general contractor during the construction, now he was acting as the plant manager, overseeing production.

Peter had two younger brothers still living in Mexico. In the early stages of the business in Mexico, his brother, Isaac worked as the interim plant manager.

Peter was needed back in Tigertown, Texas, but with up to 50 employees in Mexico he knew before he could leave they would need additional management help. He had a nephew; a bright young man in his early thirties. Also born in Mexico, he spoke German, English and Spanish fluently. If he could promote him into management it would be a perfect fit.

Peter and the Mexico management team made the offer and the young man accepted. His name was Jacobo Thiessen. With Jacobo as the new plant manager, Peter was confident that under Jacobo's leadership production would go well. At the close of the first year, **PJ Trailers** in Mexico had already made a profit.

When the plant in Mexico first started it had been Peter's plan to build only the trailer frames and then ship them to Seminole, Texas, to the **PJ Trailer** plant for final assembly. But **PJ Trailers Mexico,** was outgrowing Seminole. "Why not build finished trailers in Mexico?" Jacobo asked.

Peter Thiessen and his management team in Tigertown, had a meeting to consider Jacobo's recommendation. It was agreed; from now on the Mexican plant would ship completed trailers to the United States ready for delivery to dealers.

By the end of the second year of the new business in Mexico, **PJ Trailers** was employing 120 people. The company employees were doing a great job. With fewer government regulations, expenses were much lower, and with the tax advantages resulting from **NAFTA**, profits were higher. Starting **PJ Trailers** in Mexico had been a good decision.

Profits are important to any business. That is one of the main reasons anyone decides to go into business. Like any other good businessman, Peter Thiessen was profit driven. But there was more than just profit that motivated him. He wanted to help people improve their lives.

Peter remembered what it was like growing up in a Mennonite community. While the word "Mennonite" really describes a Christian church denomination, to him it had also been a culture and a distinct way of life. This includes clothes, food and even the mode of transportation.

He knew that even today, in Belize, Bolivia and Paraguay, there were still Mennonite colonies that held fast to the traditional old ways. He had no problem with that. If that is what they enjoyed, do it. What did concern him was when people put their religion and culture above faith in God.

While the rest of the world and specifically Americans and Canadians looked at Mennonites as people of good morals and a strong work ethic, Peter knew that Mennonites were sinners too. In his adult life he had come to realize that no matter how good you are; good works cannot earn anyone a ticket to heaven.

Eternal life only comes by faith in the finished work of Jesus Christ when he died on the cross and rose again on the third day. Peter was not a preacher; he wasn't even a deacon in his church. But he had a desire to tell others about the love, the goodness and the Grace of God.

Maybe through his business, **PJ TRAILERS** in Mexico, he could bring glory to God. People in Mexico and for that matter everywhere, need to know God's plan of Salvation; that Jesus came and died for the sins of the world and that one day he will return to take His children home to heaven.

Peter Thiessen believes that we need to take the Gospel to the world and that takes money. He knows money doesn't grow on trees. Rather, it is God blessing his children.

To enjoy God's blessing in our lives, we need to know that we are fulfilling the purpose we were created to fill. We need to do it for the benefit of other people as well as for the glory of God, our Creator.

Here are the words of Jesus spoken in Matthew 6:33; "Seek ye first the kingdom of God and all the other things will be added unto you."

Psalm 37: 4 says it this way; "Delight yourself in the Lord and he will give you the desires of your heart." Peter knows that God has blessed him, to be a blessing to others.

However, this concept is not limited to Peter and Sara Thiessen or **PJ TRAILERS.** God is not a respecter of persons. He has a plan and a purpose for each individual.

Good News and Bad News
Sara's Baby Was Having a Baby

The youngest of Peter and Sara's five children, Sarah was born in Canada. She was just six years old and in the first grade, when the family moved from Winkler, Manitoba to settle in Tigertown, Texas.

After attending the local Christian high school, Sarah was ready for her first job. Making room for their children to be employed at **PJ TRAILERS** was important to Peter. When they were ready, he did whatever it took to find the right spot for each one.

When Sarah applied for work at **PJ TRAILERS** she was accepted. Sarah would be the new Company receptionist. With her happy disposition and a charming personality, Peter knew she was the right person for the job.

The first time Sarah answered the phone and said, "Hello, this is **PJ TRAILERS,**" she felt like she had just grown up. She had a job, and that meant that she would also get a paycheck. Although the company had been doing well, still Peter wanted to make sure everyone in the family carried their share of the load and Sarah knew that as well.

Sarah's older sister Lisa and her husband, Pete Zacharias always spent time in Canada during the summer months. **PJ Trailers** had a sales office close to Winkler, Manitoba, and they were in charge of it. From time to time, Sarah had the opportunity to go there as well.

This is also where she met her future husband, Henry Friesen. He had a cousin living in Winkler who had seen Sarah and liked what he saw. He told Henry about this "hot chick" from Texas, who was in town and suggested they go and meet her. But it wasn't the cousin; it was Henry that Sarah took a liking to.

When Sarah returned to Tigertown, she brought Henry's phone number with her. If she used the company phone to call Henry, likely there was a spike in the phone bills. They talked a lot. Her mother and father knew that Sarah and Henry were getting serious when she invited him to come to Texas for a visit.

Raised in a conservative Mennonite family, Sara knew she would need to join the church, before getting married. Church membership classes at their church in Tigertown were already over for the year. But Sarah had an idea; **PJ Trailers** already had an office in Seminole, Texas and she would go and work there for a while.

Her reason; there was another church of their denomination in Seminole. She had checked and they were still having membership classes, and they were willing to accept her. With the approval of her parents, Sarah packed and was heading west for Seminole.

Their wedding day came; it was an elegant event. Her father, Peter Thiessen even got a new pair of boots and a Stetson hat to wear. She and her mother were very close, so it was a bittersweet day for her mom. Sarah was going to get married. Her baby was leaving home.

Sarah was now Mrs. Henry Friesen. But there was a problem; Henry Friesen did not have a visa or a green card so he could work in the United States. This was not a big issue for her dad's company; **PJ TRAILERS** had an office in Edmonton, Alberta, Canada. She and Henry could move to Canada and work in the Canadian division of the Company.

Here was the hurdle; moving to Canada meant being away from her family and especially her mother, and that was challenging for young Sarah. Finally she realized that their options were limited. She and Henry would need to go north for the foreseeable future, until his L-1 visa issue was resolved.

Edmonton, Alberta was two thousand miles away. "Thank God for the telephone," Sarah thought to herself. She could still talk to her mom on a regular basis. Just hearing her voice would ease the pain of being so far away from her family.

It was in July of 2004. Sarah had just come out of the doctor's office. She had good news and she had to share it with her mother. Quickly she dialed area code 903 and then her parent's number. "Mom," she shouted, "I'm pregnant." Both Sarah and her mother were so excited.

The pregnancy was going well. Sarah was in her twenty-sixth week and she went to the doctor for a regular checkup. After doing an echo-gram, the doctor came back with a devastating report. Her unborn baby had been diagnosed with **"HYPO-PLASTIC LEFT HEART SYNDROME."** It meant that the left side of the baby's heart had never formed.

The Doctor had told them they had only three options open to them. Since Sarah was past twenty one weeks in her pregnancy, he said it was too late to terminate the pregnancy. This was something Henry and Sarah would not even consider.

The Doctor continued; the first remaining option was to do nothing. After the baby was born, it would soon die a natural death.

Secondly, there were a series of surgical procedures, including open heart surgery that could possibly extend the baby's life.

The third option was for the baby to undergo a heart transplant at a later time, but still in his early childhood. None of the three proposed options offered much hope to Henry and Sarah and their baby. In addition, just the mention of pregnancy termination (abortion) was repulsive to them.

Once again Sarah dialed her mother's number, but this time her heart was broken. After sharing the news there was a long silence, as both mother and daughter cried together. "How could this happen? What did we do to deserve this?" Sarah asked herself. No one; not her parents, her friends nor her pastor had an answer.

When Sarah's father, Peter Thiessen heard about the diagnosis, he made an immediate decision. "Bring Sarah and her husband Henry back to Texas." Texas had some of the best doctors and hospitals; that is what he wanted to provide for his daughter and her new baby.

In just 90 more days the baby would be born. In addition to good medical care Sarah needed her mother. When the airliner touched down at the Dallas airport, Peter and Sara were there to meet her.

Coming from Edmonton, Canada, it had been a long trip for an expectant mother. As the car rolled into the driveway of her parents home, she was ready for a needed sleep.

In the midst of her emotional pain and the discomforts of pregnancy, Sarah was happy to be back home in Tigertown, Texas. Now she was waiting for her husband Henry to join her.

90 Days and Counting
Wishing She Could Remain Pregnant Forever

Sarah was back in Texas and her husband Henry Friesen was on his way to Dallas, Texas from Edmonton, Alberta, Canada. She had met with Dr. Wilkerson MD, an obstetrician in Paris, Texas and he had confirmed the diagnosis. Yes, her baby did have "**HYPO-PLASTIC LEFT HEART SYNDROME.**"

But there was one big difference; unlike her doctors in Edmonton, Clifton E. Wilkerson, MD never suggested or even mentioned terminating the pregnancy. Sarah soon discovered that Dr. Wilkerson himself was the father of a **DOWN'S SYNDROME** child. He valued life as much as she and Henry did.

She knew this was the kind of a doctor she and her unborn baby needed. Visiting his office, Sarah felt that she was more than just another patient. Dr. Wilkerson really cared about her and the baby she was carrying.

When Dr. Wilkerson performed the last ultrasound, he knew the sex of the baby. Sarah did not want to know it until she and Henry were together. Dr. Wilkerson understood and he wrote it down and handed her the slip of paper.

True to her word, Sarah waited until Henry Friesen had arrived on his flight from Edmonton, Alberta, Canada, before opening the note Dr. Wilkerson had written for her. She read it out loud for Henry to hear. "It's going to be a boy," Sarah squealed, but her excitement was short lived.

It was Sunday February the 20, 2005, and Henry and Sarah Friesen were on their way to Dallas, Texas. They had an important appointment to keep at the **PARKLAND HOSPITAL.** Dr. Wilkerson had made the arrangements for them.

On Monday Sarah was scheduled to give birth to their first baby. They knew it was going to be a boy. But this was not going to be just another baby boy born in Texas. Their baby would be born with only half a heart and his chances of survival were slim.

Sarah knew she was in one of the finest medical facilities in the United States, and for that matter in the world. But Sarah and her husband Henry also knew that there was a limit to what doctors and nurses at **PARKLAND** could do; they needed a miracle for their little unborn baby.

It was early Monday morning and Sarah could not sleep. She knew that in just a few more hours the labor pains would begin. Soon the nurses would begin to induce labor and the birthing process would start. She knew there would be discomfort, but she was not afraid of the pain.

Her concern was for her little baby who was resting so comfortably inside her. She knew that as long as he was inside her body, her heart was keeping him alive and well. Recently she had even enjoyed the little kicks she felt against her stomach wall. Sometimes she had wished she could just remain pregnant forever.

During the past months Sarah had learned to appreciate the support of her family and especially her wonderful husband Henry. Right now all she wanted was to have Henry by her side holding her hand. As the minutes turned into hours, they were both glad that they had faith in a living God, who loved them and cared for them, even if at the moment life didn't make sense.

By now Sarah's parents, Peter and Sara Thiessen had arrived and were in the hospital waiting room. Henry's mother, Anna Friesen, had also flown in from her home in the country of Belize. Considering the doctor's serious prognosis, Henry's mom wanted to be there just in case the baby did not live.

It had been a long day in the waiting room, but it was much longer for Sarah and Henry. When they saw the doctors and nurses and other medical technicians running in and out of the room, they knew it was close.

The medical team was getting ready to move the new born infant from the safety of its mother's womb into the **INTENSIVE CARE UNIT AT THE PARKLAND CHILDREN'S HOSPITAL.**

As Sarah put it; at 8:45 PM her little baby boy was tired of being in his mother's tummy. It was time to get out. One final push and her little son was born. When the umbilical cord was severed her little baby had to make it on his own.

One of the attending nurses took the baby and placed it into Sarah's waiting arms. She held him to her breast for a moment. He was her first baby and he was still alive. Sarah and Henry had decided to call him Elijah. In the Bible, Elijah had been a man of miracles. This was the right name for their baby. He would need a miracle too.

Quickly Elijah was rushed into the **HOSPITAL ICU** and put on life support. It had been nine months since Sarah got pregnant, and the last three months had been extremely hard. Finally it was over. Sarah had done all she could do. Now it was up to God and the medical staff at Parkland working together to keep her baby alive.

Little Elijah was in **ICU** at the hospital. Now it seemed like no one was in a hurry to release Sarah. All she wanted to do is to be with her baby. The children's hospital section was a good distance away, so every day, her husband Henry would come and roll her wheelchair down the aisle to the **ICU**. But all they could do was look at him.

It seemed that even light conversation seemed to bother him and would set off alarms on the monitors and other electrical devices attached. At a point she could not stand it anymore; she told Henry that she was willing to have everything disconnected from his little body and let him pass away, rather than see him suffer anymore.

After five days Sarah was released from Parkland Hospital. While the rest of the family returned to their respective homes, Henry and Sarah decided to stay in Dallas. Her father Peter Thiessen had rented a suite of rooms at the Embassy Hotel where they and other family members could stay.

Elijah was just ten days old when they did his first open heart surgery. It was called the **NORWOOD PROCEDURE.** After five and a half more weeks in the hospital Sarah and Henry finally took their baby home!

It was only a few short years before Elijah would need his second surgery. As he came out of the operating room, there was a lot of bleeding. By three o'clock in the morning the doctors called Henry and Sarah.

They needed to redo the surgery and asked them to come and sign parental consent forms. This time everything went well and soon the little family was back at home.

It was seven more weeks at home before Elijah slowly learned how to walk again. He had been lying on the couch for weeks, not having the energy to even walk to the kitchen table. When he finally began feeling better, to celebrate the occasion, the entire Thiessen family, including grandpa and grandma, took a vacation to Disney World.

After just one day at the park, Sarah noticed a lot of swelling on Elijah. She knew immediately that something was very wrong. The vacation was cut short and Elijah was rushed back to the hospital in Dallas, Texas. At this point the doctors told Henry and Sarah that the only hope for Elijah's survival was a heart transplant.

On July 7, 2009 Elijah was put on the heart transplant list. The doctors told Henry and Sarah that without a transplant, Elijah might not make it to the end of the year.

They knew that the chances of a donor heart becoming available for a young child were not very good. But they had no option. All they had left, was to pray and to wait. Even praying sometimes seemed difficult as the days slipped away.

At those times Henry and Sarah were glad they had each other to lean on. They were also happy to be part of a loving church family. Everyone else in the church knew about Elijah and his need for a new heart. They also knew that soon time for a transplant would be running out.

Thank God!
And God Bless Mary Jane

Peter and Sara Thiessen and their family were all aware that five-year-old Elijah was now on an official heart transplant list. But they also knew that unless a heart donor became available soon, Elijah likely would not live beyond the coming New Year.

As Elijah's parents, Henry and Sarah had been given a pager to alert them immediately, should a matched heart become available. It was exciting but at the same time it was scary. A heart transplant is very complicated. They knew it was going to be a high risk procedure. With a pager on the night stand, for a couple of nights, going to bed was not easy for the anxious young mom and dad.

The doctors had told them that it would be a good idea to have a suitcase packed and ready at all times, just in case they received a call. Everywhere Elijah went, the pager also had to go and he was never to go anywhere by himself.

Month after month Henry and Sarah had to take Elijah to the clinic for a checkup. Doctors wanted to keep a closer eye on how his weak heart was doing. The sad news was that with each visit, his heart was slowly getting worse.

In July of 2010 the doctors decided it was time to put a PICC-Line into Elijah's heart. This would allow them to inject medicine directly into his heart to keep it functioning. They were doing everything they could to keep him alive until a donor heart for transplant became available.

The waiting was hard! The Friesen family could never leave the Paris, Texas area. At all times they had to be within two hours of the hospital, should they get a call on the pager. Now with the PICC-Line attached, Elijah had even more restrictions. He was no longer allowed to swim in the swimming pool.

On October 2, 2010 at 7:50 PM they got the call. It was their transplant coordinator Nashawn calling Sarah's cell phone. All Sarah heard was "Hey Sarah, it's Nashawn here." A poor cell phone reception had dropped the call. Immediately Henry's cell phone started ringing. All that Sarah heard Henry say is "Ok, we will get our bags ready and be on our way."

Henry came out of the bedroom screaming, "They have a heart available for Elijah." For a moment, Henry and Sarah stood there hugging and crying. It was hard for them to believe that a heart transplant was going to be happening to Elijah very soon.

Elijah saw their mixed emotions and ran into his room crying. He told his parents that he didn't want a new heart. Sarah reminded him that with a new heart, he would be able to play sports like he always wanted. Elijah forced a smile, but they could tell there were a lot of things going through his little mind.

Henry and Sarah asked Elijah to come and join them. Before they left the house and headed for the hospital, they wanted to pray for the donor family that had just said their last goodbye to a loved one.

As the little family held hands, they also prayed that everything would go well with Elijah and the major surgery he was going to go through, when they got to the hospital in Dallas, Texas.

Sarah made a quick call to her parents and told them about the call from the transplant coordinator. By now Sarah was frantically running from room to room not knowing what to take or what to leave. By 8:30 they were on their way. Sarah held little Elijah in her arms all the way.

She continued to pray for Elijah, asking God to make him strong. Then Sarah prayed for the doctors and the medical team that was going to operate on her little boy in just a few hours. Elijah was very quiet all the way to the hospital in Dallas, Texas.

Still on the road, the transplant coordinator called Sarah and reminded her that Elijah was not supposed to eat or drink anything from this point on. Sarah asked Nashawn if the heart was already at the hospital. She told Sarah it was not, and that there were a lot of things that still had to be done to prepare for the transplant.

While Henry drove, Sarah continued making call after call. She was telling everyone she knew what was going on and asked them to pray. They were almost at the hospital and Elijah said, "Mommy, pray for me one more time." As she finished her prayer, suddenly Sarah and Henry felt a calmness they could not explain.

It was now 10:30 PM and they had just arrived at the hospital. Henry dropped Sarah and Elijah off at the front door, while he went and parked the car. Perhaps out of nervousness, both Sarah and Elijah needed to use the rest-room.

Elijah was already finished and was waiting on his mother. Impatiently he said, "Mom, you'd better hurry or they may start the transplant without me." It seemed so funny, Sarah burst out laughing. Then she assured him that the doctors would definitely wait for him.

By now Henry had come in and was ready to take them up to the third floor and into the heart Intensive Care Unit. Everyone was excited to see that Elijah had arrived. That evening everyone was giving him the royal treatment. He loved all the attention and then proceeded to show the nurses where in his chest, they needed to put this new heart.

It was time to hook him up to the various heart monitors and the Pulse Oximeter machine and start with the Pre-op tests that needed to be done. Sarah's parents had not arrived yet, but she was so grateful that two of her older brothers,

Frank and Jake had come to be with them for the big surgery that was soon going to begin. Doctors were telling them that surgery might not start until three or four in the morning. Sarah and Henry were shocked that it was going to take that long.

What they did not know at the time; the heart is the last organ that can be harvested from a donor and there were more than thirty other recipients waiting in line.

It must have been 2:00 in the morning when Elijah finally fell asleep. Lying next to him was Sarah, his mother. "What if my boy doesn't make it out of the operating room?" she wondered. It seemed repetitive, but once again she prayed for Elijah. It was an extremely long and hard night and one she will never forget.

It was 4:00 in the morning when the nurses came to give Elijah his first dose of anti-rejection medicine. At 5:00 the surgical team came to get him. Sarah and Henry had been waiting for this moment for a long time. Still, it was one of the hardest things they would ever go through.

As they walked Elijah down the hall to the operating room, Sarah knew the time had come the time to say good-bye. She hugged him and told him how much she loved him. Elijah looked like he was still sleeping, but suddenly his little eyes opened wide and full of tears. "Mommy, I'm scared!" he said. Sarah didn't want him to know, but she was scared too.

What was she supposed to do? She felt like taking him and running away. But then she also knew his old heart was extremely sick! There comes a time in life, when you simply have to trust God. At that moment, Sarah knew she had reached that point.

Elijah had asked if Daddy could walk with him into the operating room. With the doctors' permission they dressed Henry in a bunny suit (at least that's what Elijah called it) and together, father and son walked the last steps.

It didn't take long and Henry came out and said that the anesthetic had quickly put Elijah to sleep. Henry and Sarah knew that the day of the transplant was going to be very long!

They were given frequent updates by the medical team of how it was going in the operating room. Sarah sent her camera into the operating room with the transplant coordinator. She had told her to get as many pictures as possible.

It was around 11:35 in the morning when the new heart arrived at the hospital. Early in the afternoon Nashawn brought Sarah her camera. It had amazing pictures of the old heart as well as the new one! Nashawn told them that sometimes a heart needs to be tickled or shocked to get it started. Elijah's new heart had started on its own.

6:30 that night, the nurses finally wheeled Elijah out of the operating room. Henry and Sarah met them in the hallway. Their precious little son finally had pink lips and pink finger tips! He was so beautiful! Never before had they seen him look so good. The nurses brought him to a room in the **ICU** and got him settled. After about an hour Sarah and Henry were able to be with him.

He was asleep but they couldn't stop looking at the heart monitors. His new heart was beating perfectly. One more time Henry and Sarah held hands and prayed. This time it was a prayer of thanksgiving. It had been a long hard day and now it was time for them to get some sleep as well.

Elijah's recovery was remarkable. He was alert with a minimum of discomfort, even on the first day. The second day after his surgery Elijah said that he wanted to go to a drive-thru restaurant and then go home. Sarah knew he was getting back to normal.

Now it was time to walk. On the third day as he took his first steps, he didn't make it very far, but step by step, day by day he was improving. Sarah and Henry needed to learn about all the new medications Elijah would need. Twenty-four pills in the morning and twenty-four pills each night was a lot of pills for a five-year-old to take on a daily basis.

After two and a half weeks the day came for Henry and Sarah to take their brand new boy home. What an exciting day! As they loaded Elijah into the car, they remembered the day they had brought him for the heart transplant. What a difference! Their hearts were singing as they headed back home to Paris, Texas.

Taking care of a heart transplant recipient was going to be a demanding task. It would be a full time project. That was not a problem for Sarah. Elijah would need three checkups a week at the hospital in Dallas.

For the first three months after the transplant, Elijah was housebound. At times he didn't understand why he just had to sit at home and do nothing. He has so much energy; he wanted to be outside doing all the things he had not been able to do before.

Going through this ordeal had not been easy for anyone, and especially Elijah. There were times when Henry and Sarah thought, "Is this the right thing to do?" But seeing him enjoy his new life, they knew it was worth it! He had a whole life ahead of him.

April 17, 2011 was another exciting day. Sarah and Henry Friesen and their family would have the opportunity to meet the mother who had donated the heart for Elijah. Usually it takes much longer before the donor and recipient families are ready to meet.

It was a big surprise that it would happen so soon. What an emotional day! The meeting was scheduled to take place in Temple, Texas. When Henry and Sarah and their family arrived, the donor's family was already there.

The donor heart had come from a ten-year-old boy, named Matthew. Matthew's mother, Mary Jane and her family were sitting in the waiting room. It was a rather somber moment and no one knew just what to expect.

After being introduced, Mary Jane got down to Elijah's level and they hugged each other. As she held him, Elijah told her, "Thank you for my new heart." A special invisible bond seemed to be forming between them. Everyone else watching, stood by speechless during this seemingly sacred moment.

Then Mary Jane asked if she could listen to her son, Matthew's heart, now beating inside of little Elijah. In anticipation of this moment, she had brought a stethoscope. Placing the listening apparatus in her ears, she gently held the chest piece to his heart. Tears welled up in her eyes, as she heard the thumps of what used to be Matthew's heart.

Now it was time for two loving mothers to meet. Sarah and Mary Jane stood there silently as they embraced. No need for words; tears were telling the story of both joy and pain. Repeatedly Sarah whispered "Thank you" to Mary Jane.

It was time for Sara's family to learn why Matthew's heart had become available. Matthew had been a healthy young boy of ten. Full of life, he enjoyed sports. Just that day he had been out playing with other boys. At bed time, Matthew had complained of a headache to his mother Mary Jane.

The next morning she had found him, lying unconscious on the floor. Immediately she knew that something was very wrong. Soon the flashing lights of the ambulance were in her driveway. They took Matthew to the nearest hospital and he was placed on life support.

Then he was life-flighted to the **Scott and White Hospital** in Temple, Texas. When Mary Jane received the doctor's evaluation and prognosis, she knew that her son Matthew was not going to make it. She was all alone, faced with life and death decisions.

Sitting there in that hospital room, suddenly Mary Jane thought of organ donating. She had never even considered becoming an organ donor herself. Now she was thinking about giving away her precious son's organs. As she spoke to the doctor about it, she was getting a fast education.

Mary Jane discovered that it is not only the heart, the kidneys, the liver and eyes that can be transplanted. With her permission, literally dozens of other children could be affected by the donation of Matthew's organs. She made the decision; she was going to do it.

Mary Jane had been given a stack of papers to read and sign. Her signature would release her son's organs to a host of other waiting recipients. It seemed like a blur, but she knew she was doing the right thing. Later on Mary Jane was told that her act of kindness had helped save the lives of about thirty other children.

As Sarah and Mary Jane said "Good-bye" they knew they would see each other again. Few others would ever understand what these two special mothers were feeling.

Once more the story took a dramatic turn. In July of 2011, **MAKE-A-WISH FOUNDATION** granted Elijah Friesen and his family his wish of visiting Disney World one more time.

Just days after a wonderful vacation, Elijah was taken to the hospital in Dallas for a routine heart transplant checkup. As he came out of the anesthesia, complications began to develop and ultimately his heart stopped beating and Elijah passed away.

You can read the rest of this heart touching story in the book titled, **"LOVE IS IN THE HEART."**

The Joy of Doing an Audit
Like Giving the Business an Enema

It was 2005. **PJ TRAILERS**, the company that had started as a mom and pop operation 15 years ago had grown into an international company. With its headquarters in the small town of Tigertown, Texas, **PJ TRAILERS** now had manufacturing plants in various other locations.

This included Seminole, Texas and Cuauhtémoc, Mexico, as well as several sales offices in Canada. A total of 750 employees were building a trailer every seven minutes, around the clock, six days a week. Total annual sales from the 45,000 trailers manufactured exceeded $100,000,000.

No longer were trailer deliveries made with single axle trucks and trailers; by now **PJ TRAILERS** owned a fleet of 45 tractor trailers. Crisscrossing America from east to west, going north to Edmonton, Alberta, Canada and then heading south to Mexico; they were delivering **PJ TRAILERS.**

The bank line of credit that had started at just one hundred thousand dollars now was up to $10 million. But even that was not enough to handle the rapid growth of the company. **PJ Trailers** needed more cash for product inventory for its ever increasing sales volume.

The company was profitable and on a good financial foundation and the bank knew it. But to fund its growth it needed an increased line of credit approaching $30 million. For that much money the bank examiners asked for a company-wide audit.

Nobody enjoys audits. But for the health of the company and its future growth, it was time to look at every aspect of the operation. This would include property, inventory, liabilities, recorded sales, accounts receivables and anything else that had to do with **PJ Trailers.**

Audits are expensive. While many Certified Public Accounts in the United States can do an audit, **PJ Trailers** had to hire an actual auditing firm. From real estate property values, to accounts receivable, inventory and accounts payable; every detail was going to be examined.

Doug Clark and his accounting firm, **Cooper Bergman,** from Dallas, Texas was in charge of the **PJ Trailer Company** audit. For the next year his accountants would be examining the records of the company to certify that things were as they appeared and then issue a report on their findings.

Most business audits are alike, but unlike an IRS audit, these auditors were not looking for tax violations or company wrongdoings. The purpose of this audit was to confirm to the bank, that **PJ Trailers** was in fact as strong financially as stated on its monthly financial statements.

From the day that Doug Clark and his audit team arrived they knew that they were among friends. Everything was open for inspection. Whatever information or records they needed, **PJ Trailers** management promptly provided.

Another thing that Doug soon discovered was Peter Thiessen's uncanny ability to recall numbers. Ask him what trailer sales were in any given year, or what **PJ TRAILERS** paid for a certain piece of equipment; Peter knew it.

The Company had state of the art computers, but Peter's only electronic tool was his small pocket calculator. Just because he didn't read or write, did not mean that Peter didn't know the profit and loss position of the Company.

Although he had almost no formal education, he could add, subtract, multiply and divide, and calculate percentages in his mind accurately. Better than a computer hard drive, his mind never needed to be backed up.

In addition to inventory, receivables, expense accounts and other profit related items, auditors also look at percentages and the cost of doing business. Two factors of interest to anyone looking at the **PJ TRAILERS** financial statements were advertising and warranty claims.

In its beginning **PJ TRAILERS** did no advertising. It was the high quality of the trailers and the very competitive pricing that attracted the dealers to carry their brand. Even when annual sales exceeded $100,000,000, the company's advertising budget was less than 1% of sales.

The same thing applied to the warranty claims department. **PJ TRAILERS** were well built and the company had minimal warranty problems. Peter enjoys telling the story of a stacked trailer coming loose during delivery and landing in the ditch with no damage other than some minor paint abrasion.

Although it was not part of the audit, Doug soon recognized the loyalty of **PJ TRAILERS** employees. But as the financial audit trail revealed, employees and especially supervisors and shop managers were well paid and also received generous bonuses. That was how Peter built company loyalty.

As an example, one year **PJ Trailers** had done very well financially and was showing a good profit margin. Without a previous commitment or obligation, Peter Thiessen himself went to Lowry Chevrolet – Cadillac in Paris, Texas. He purchased 14 new Chevrolet, crew pickup trucks and gave one to each of the shift supervisors for Christmas.

In due course the audit was completed and presented to the bank. **PJ Trailers** paid a hefty fee to Doug Clark and the audit firm and the bank filed the audit under **PJ Trailers**. The end result was that the bank was able to increase the company line of credit to $28,000,000. Not bad for a guy who didn't read or write and only uses a pocket calculator.

But that was not the end of the story. Doug Clark, who had overseen the audit, recognized the value of **PJ Trailers** as a company. He knew a group of financial investors who were looking to purchase a profitable company. He thought **PJ Trailers** might be just what they wanted.

As someone who had just completed a thorough company audit, his recommendation carried a lot of weight. When the time was right, Doug knew he was going to talk to Peter Thiessen about selling **PJ Trailers** to this investment group.

Willing to Sell the Company
And Someone Willing to Make an Offer

The audit was over. The company now had a line of credit of $28,000,000 and the future looked brighter than ever before. The small company that started with Peter, his two sons Peter Jr., and Jake, now had 750 employees.

No hard decisions today; until the phone rang. It was Doug Clark, the guy who headed up the audit that the bank had requested. "Peter, this is Doug; when can I have a meeting with you? I think you and your family may be interested in what I have to tell you."

"Is there something wrong?" Peter wanted to know. "No, everything is fine, but I have an idea I want to present to you. When can we meet?" Doug insisted. Peter had come to know Doug and he trusted him. Before the call ended they had selected a date for the proposed meeting.

As the day of the meeting arrived, Peter kept wondering what Doug Clark could have on his mind. He wasn't worried; just curious. Peter, his sons Jake and Frank, and sons-in-law Pete Zacharias and Henry Friesen were all seated at the conference table when Doug walked in.

After the normal small talk, Doug got right to the point. "Peter, what do you think your company, **PJ TRAILERS** is worth?" This was something Peter never really had thought about. To him the Company was like a machine that built trailers and made money.

It didn't matter to him what it was worth. He didn't plan to sell it. Just keep it working, was his way of thinking. Doug wanted an answer, so he asked the question again. Peter wondered what Doug had in mind. Without even giving it a serious thought, Peter said, "Maybe twelve million dollars."

The company had annual sales that exceeded a hundred million dollars. He knew Peter was not serious. Doug continued; "Would you sell the company for fifty million dollars?" he asked.

"No," was Peter's reply. "How about sixty million?" Again "No." "Seventy five million?" Still "No." Doug decided it was time to tell Peter Thiessen and his family, why he had asked for the meeting.

Having done the recent audit, Doug Clark knew more about **PJ TRAILERS** than Peter or anyone else on the management team. Doug explained to them that he had a possible buyer for **PJ TRAILERS COMPANY**. It was a financial investment group from Dallas, Texas.

If they could come to terms with Peter and his family, they were willing to make a cash offer. Peter was overwhelmed. He was not ready to make this big a decision quickly. First of all, **PJ TRAILERS** was not his Company. Years ago he had given it to God. He was just the manager.

Since it was God's company, he would have to first ask him, before he could sell it to Doug's investment group. He would also have to talk to Sara and the rest of the family. Peter and his family had built this business together. They were a part of the Company and their input was important to him.

Peter, Sara and their children as well as their spouses would have to be in agreement on the decision. "I need to pray about this; our family needs to talk about it and then we will make a decision. We need ten days," Peter concluded. "In ten days we will tell you what the company is worth, and if we will even consider selling it to your investors."

As they left the meeting, everyone in the Thiessen family seemed to be in a daze. They had never imagined that this day would come. There was actually a group of investors who were waiting to pay millions and millions of dollars for something they had helped to create with their bare hands.

Peter needed to be alone. He had to talk to God, but he didn't really know where to begin. When things were tough most of the time he had been asking God for money. This time he needed to know if he should take the money that was being offered to him.

These numbers were so big, he wasn't sure anyone else in the family really knew the magnitude of the decision they were facing. One thing Peter was sure of; these numbers were not too big for God. He needed God's wisdom to make this important decision.

As much as Peter liked doing business and enjoyed making money, within his heart, he had a fear of being rich. He remembered what money had done in his father's life. Although his dad, Jake Thiessen was never overly wealthy, there had been years in his life when he had made a lot more money than what he needed to support his family.

In those times, he had seen his father lose his sense of morality and good judgment. Like an immature teenager, his middle-aged father had acted foolishly and indulged in what was not good and wholesome. Peter was afraid that if he became rich, this might also happen to him.

Alone, on his knees, Peter bared his heart to God. He needed to know, "Should we sell, or should we keep the company?" He even told God about his fear of being rich. Now it was God's turn to speak, so Peter became silent. He had asked for direction; now he was willing to listen.

In a still small voice, God reminded Peter that He was the one who had blessed **PJ TRAILERS.** Peter had given it to God but He needed Peter and Sara to handle the checkbook.

"To sell or not to sell?" there was no immediate answer. Often it seems that God is not in a hurry to respond. But as Peter and Sara and their family discussed the offer, Peter felt a peace in his heart. Could it be that there were other things God wanted them to do in the days ahead?

"Maybe the price should be a hundred million;" Sara and the family left those negotiations up to Peter. He was the one who had started the company, he had given it to God, and God would have to let Peter know whether to accept or reject the investors final offer. The family had one more meeting.

Their minds were made up. Peter and his family agreed they would accept between eighty-five million and one hundred million dollars for their company. This would include the manufacturing plants in the United States and Mexico. But it excluded the Canadian operation.

Selling a company of this size was more complicated than Peter had expected. Both the buyer and the seller had to have legal representation. Once again appraisers and accountants got involved. The final result; **PJ TRAILERS** was purchased by Doug's investment group.

Being a private company, the final negotiated price will remain confidential. As Peter and his family walked away from the Company they had built; it was a bittersweet moment. For twenty years **PJ TRAILERS** had been their home. What would they do now? They were all unemployed. It was time to take a vacation.

Peter knew that there would be other and even bigger opportunities in the family's future. All they needed to do was **LISTEN, DECIDE AND OBEY.**

Note:

Doug Clark is the new President/CEO of **PJ TRAILERS MFG CO. INC.**, located at 1807 on Farm to Market Rd #2352, 2 miles west of Tigertown, Texas. The company continues to build each trailer with the same attention to detail that has made **PJ TRAILERS** the workhorse that hard working professionals count on to do their jobs.

After the completion of the sale of **PJ TRAILERS,** the CEO of the Investment Group, Douglas D. Wheat, together with his top management team, had one more meeting with Peter Thiessen.

"What is the secret of your business success with **PJ TRAILERS?**" Doug asked. "There must be something I do not understand." "Do you really want to know?" Peter replied. Doug was waiting for the anticipated answer.

"Every morning I get down on my knees and ask God for his help and blessing. Then, every night; again on my knees, I thank Him for answering my prayer."

Doug Wheat had one more request: "Will you continue to pray for." **PJ TRAILERS?**" He asked. "Yes!" Was Peter's simple answser. By the Grace of God, Peter has been able to keep his promise.

The Family Business
It All Started as A Mom & Pop Operation

Working together as a family has many benefits, but it can also become challenging, both in hard times and in good times. It would be foolish to pretend that Peter and Sara Thiessen were model parents or that they had a perfect family and there never were any problems

Since the beginning of time, there have been no perfect families; including the first family, Adam and Eve. Here the first son murdered the second son. It may not have been intentional, but still Cain's angry act resulted in the death of the younger brother Abel.

No human being, outside of Jesus, has ever lived a perfect life, and that includes Peter and Sara Thiessen. But imperfection is not a license to be selfish or rude. In the Mennonite tradition, trying to keep the family close was very important but it never is easy.

Only after they had been married for some 15 years, did Peter and Sara come into a fuller understanding of having a personal relationship with God. Something Peter had learned the hard way was asking for forgiveness, first from God and then from those he had offended.

Whether it was with an individual like his wife, or a group of people, like the church leadership, Peter had humbled himself to say, "I was wrong in my attitude or actions. I am sorry, will you forgive me?" This was a spiritual truth Peter and Sara practiced and tried to instill in their children as well.

As their children got married and brought new in-laws into the family, it became more difficult, but still they heard Peter talking about the importance of admitting when you are wrong, and asking and receiving forgiveness from the offended party.

In many of the Old Colony families, and this included Peter and Sara, family prayers were limited to saying a table grace. Asking God's blessing before the meal and a word of thanksgiving after was about the only time children actually heard their parents pray.

What the children knew about Peter and Sara was that they prayed often in their private lives. In the morning, on their knees before the day began and again at night, before going to bed, they knew Mom and Dad were praying for them.

It seemed natural for Mennonite family members to work together on the farm. Now Peter and Sara tried to implement the idea of their family working together in the business as well. As each of the Thiessen children grew older, it was expected and accepted that they would also work in the family business, at least when they were young.

Peter had short names for the businesses he started. As a matter of fact, some of his earlier businesses did not have an official name. It was simply Peter Thiessen doing business and making money. (Or trying to make money)

When they started the trailer manufacturing company in Tigertown, Texas in 1991, Peter named the company **PJ TRAILERS**. P & J, were the initials of Peter and Jake, their first two sons. Somehow, with a Mennonite background, having the initials of the daughters included in the name of the business just didn't fit.

But times were changing, and as they got older, the girls in the Thiessen family got involved in the business as well. The business name may not have changed, but as parents, Peter and Sara knew the contribution that each of the children was making to the business in their respective roles in the Company.

They may not all have had the same strength, but they were all a part of the family business. However, early on in the business it didn't matter who had what ability. The emphasis was on getting the job done. And by the way, everyone had the ability to help keep the place clean and everyone was expected to do their part.

While the company had four employees when it started; there really was only one person on the payroll and that was Robert Fults. Everyone else was family and was expected to work to earn their daily bread. If you were able to work, there was never any free lunch in the Thiessen household.

One of the most willing workers at **PJ TRAILERS** was Peter Jr. Being the oldest of the children he knew it was expected of him, but he did it without complaining. Hours didn't matter to him. Some days it was from sun up to midnight. If there were trailers to be built, you could count on Peter Jr, to be on the job.

At the time of move, when Peter and Sara came to Texas, Lisa, their second child and oldest daughter, had asked to stay in Canada to finish her high school in Winkler, Manitoba. When she graduated, she too came to Tigertown, Texas to live with the rest of her family.

Early on in the business, Peter kept most of the accounting numbers in his head. Although he has an exceptional memory, it soon reached its limitations. It was time to set up the books for the company and begin data entry and data processing.

Lisa, who had just finished high school at the time, knew more about computers than anyone else in the family. That meant that her job would be in the accounting department. As described in an earlier chapter, at her father's request and to help the business she and her boyfriend Pete Zacharias, agreed to a 90 day delay in their wedding plans.

On a side note; Peter likes things to be neat and clean. That includes the grass and shrubbery around the house. As the business continued to grow, Peter and Sara decided to build a bigger and nicer home. The yard was fenced and had a planted hedge growing along the outside.

Peter had gone to town and left orders for the boys, Texas Pete, Jake and Frank to cut the hedges. When he returned he was not satisfied with their effort. Rather than scold them, he decided to show them the right way to trim hedges. This was a lesson they would always remember.

Being somewhat short of stature, Peter backed his Cadillac Escalade up to the hedge and used the back tailgate for a step. Soon he was standing on the edge of the tailgate and leaning over, as he continued to prune the top of the hedge. Reaching for the outer edge, suddenly he felt he was losing his balance, but it was too late.

Dropping the cutting shears, his hat flying in the opposite direction, Peter fell head first into the prickly row of shrubs. Being short tempered by nature, the adrenalin kicked in. Once back up on his feet, Peter got back into the Cadillac and casually parked it on the driveway.

At this point he was more concerned about who had seen him than the condition of the hedge. He discovered there had been no witnesses. Still the story was too funny, not to tell the family what had happened.

As **PJ TRAILERS** continued to grow, there were many non-family employees added. Still when there were difficult positions to fill or if emergency situations arose, Peter looked to his family members to assume those responsibilities.

Peter had never lacked confidence in himself and had the same feeling of confidence in each of his children. Even though they may have lacked experience, he was willing to trust them and to them this was just being a part of the Peter Thiessen family.

Jake, the middle son in the family, had an analytical mind. He liked to figure out what makes things work. This was also true in the field of computer programs. Operating in various locations, Jake knew that the computers needed to be able to talk to each other in a network.

Judy Klassen, who later became Jake's wife, was born and grew up in Seminole, Texas. After she and Jake married, like everyone else in the Thiessen family, she began working for the company. From receptionist to accounts receivable, from office manager to janitor, Judy quickly became part of the **PJ TRAILERS** team.

PJ TRAILERS needed to implement new inventory controls, but with different programs in each location, it was chaotic. Jake knew that relying on computer consultants can be costly and time consuming. As he listened to what the programmers were saying, he began to understand how programs are written.

At the time, Jake was working at the Seminole, Texas location, but Tigertown needed him. Jake took a Redwing accounting program and together with his programmer, adapted it to handling accounting and inventory tasks that had been termed, "impossible."

Titles were never the big thing at **PJ TRAILERS**; it was performance. Whoever was the president or vice president; and whoever was the controller or the Chief Operations Officer didn't matter. What mattered was getting the job done and doing it right.

While the employees may not have known what a **CEO** really was, everyone at the business knew that Peter Thiessen was the Chief.

Frank, Jake's younger brother and the fourth in the family liked to talk. Where Jake was quiet and contemplative, Frank was loud and impulsive. But even talkative Frank began his career on the factory floor doing whatever needed to be done.

Pete Zacharias, Lisa's husband, had moved from Canada and assumed the role of general manager. At the same time, **PJ Trailers, Canada** was growing and so Pete also spent considerable time there. During those times Frank, who was in his early twenties, was asked to assume management duties.

This was not a problem unless an emergency decision had to be made. Seldom a day, and never a month went by, where the company did not face an emergency of one kind or another. It might be personnel or it could be product orders, but the worst challenges were financial ones.

Peter Thiessen was in Mexico setting up the **PJ Trailers** factory. He had asked for parts of every kind to be shipped from the Tigertown location. Inventory that had been delivered to Mexico was being billed to Tigertown. Vendors were asking for payment, and the funds were not in the bank.

It was time to talk to Dad and Frank placed the call. Sell more trailers, was Peter's quick solution. He knew there was lots of inventory, all they needed was sales. Give bigger discounts and let dealers know we are in a cash bind. They will help us, he told Frank. Frank knew that arguing with his father would not work. All he could do was to begin calling **PJ Trailer** dealers.

Frank picked up the phone and began dialing. It was only a matter of days until the financial dilemma was solved. In less than a week, Frank had sold over two million dollars of **PJ Trailers**. There was one call that Frank, or for that matter Peter will never forget.

Frank had called one of their well known dealers and told him about **PJ TRAILERS** momentary financial challenge. They had done lots of business before and they knew each other well. Still, when the dealer offered to send Frank a check of over a half million dollars, ($500,000 plus) as advance payment for trailers; Frank about dropped the phone.

This was a deal even his father Peter could not have made. Frank knew that somehow God was involved in **PJ TRAILERS**. Not one to compliment employees a lot, Peter's "I knew you could do it," was all Frank needed to hear. It made him proud to be part of the Peter Thiessen family.

There were several reasons worth mentioning that made this transaction possible. First, the dealer Frank called had the resources to make the generous offer to prepay his trailer purchases. Secondly, **PJ TRAILERS** had a sterling reputation and a trustworthy relationship with their dealers. Lastly, it was the blessing of God on **PJ TRAILERS**, the company Peter Thiessen had given to God years earlier.

"Mother" Sara Thiessen never worked at **PJ TRAILERS** as an employee. That didn't mean she was not involved. She was Peter's closest advisor and she knew how to get his attention. When they married they had promised each other; "for better or for worse." She had already seen the "for worse," now she was enjoying the "for better," time.

Peter was out of town and Sara was alone in the house when there was a knock on the door. It was an employee telling her that someone was stealing trailer parts from trailers parked on the lot. Not knowing what to do, she gave their son Jake his instructions.

"Go out on the trailer lot to see if there is someone there. If you see anything, come and tell me and we can call the police." Jake was scared, but he was more afraid to let his mother know how scared he was. Minutes seemed like hours. When he finally returned he had seen nothing unusual.

Weeks later the thief was discovered. The guilty party was the employee who had come to report the theft. Reporting it to Sara had merely been a decoy to provide cover for what he was doing. After all, he had cared enough to let Sara know about the thief on the lot. As the episode came to a close, Jake reminded Peter and Sara that night watchman was not on his list of duties.

Sarah was the youngest and the last one in the family to join the staff at **PJ TRAILERS**. By the time she came to work there were hundreds of other employees. Obviously she wasn't going to be a welder and Lisa was already involved in the bookkeeping. Sarah had a sweet voice and a pretty smile. Peter thought she would be a good receptionist.

Not only was the business growing, so was the family. Lisa had married Pete Zacharias and he was now involved in management of **PJ TRAILERS**. Pete was considerably older than either Jake or Frank, and was a definite asset in dealing with other much older Company employees.

Frank, still a teenager, had fallen in love with a Canadian girl. Her name was Darcy Penner. Big problem: she didn't speak Low German and most of the other employees did. Also, growing up in Canada, she was not as conservative as most of the other girls in the local church.

Marrying someone who was an "outsider" did not sit well with the church leadership in Tigertown, Texas. But Frank loved Darcy Penner more than he loved the church elders. Following the example of his father and mother, Frank and his sweetheart Darcy got married in Canada.

When Frank and Darcy settled in Texas, they had become family. Soon Darcy became an employee of **PJ TRAILERS**. She managed both the accounts receivable and accounts payable for the company. It no long mattered that she didn't speak Low German. After all, numbers are the same in any language.

Henry Friesen was the newest kid on the block. He was the most traveled person in the Thiessen clan. Born in Belize, he had lived in Canada, moved back to Belize, back to Canada and finally he was in Texas. After Henry and Sarah Friesen married, they moved back to Canada where he managed **PJ TRAILERS** in Edmonton Alberta.

Finally, with an L-1 visa in hand, Henry and Sarah moved back to Texas. By now **PJ TRAILERS** had become a huge operation. The company owned 45 tractor trailers that delivered **PJ TRAILERS** nationwide, as well as to Canada and Mexico. Henry assumed the responsibility of dispatcher, scheduling the pick up and deliveries of **PJ TRAILERS** to and from dealers.

It was time for Sarah and Henry to have a baby. This was going to be a bittersweet experience. There was great joy when Sarah discovered she was expecting. But sweet became bitter, at least for the moment, when they got the diagnosis that the baby had only half a heart.

As you read the chapter titled "**GOOD NEWS – BAD NEWS**" you will walk with the Thiessen family as they go through the valley of the shadow of death. Spending time with Henry and Sarah Friesen as little Elijah is given a new heart, is a heart touching experience you will never forget.

In the writing of this book, each family member has been asked, "What was the secret to success for **PJ TRAILERS?**"

Without exception, each one in their own words has said, "We were a family." "We built the best trailers and dealers liked them." "Dad gets lots of credit," and so on. Finally each family member recognizes, "**PJ TRAILERS** could not have happened without the help of God."

Take Care of Your Employees

And They Will Take Care Of You!

With the exception of their two sons Peter Jr. and Jake, Robert Fults was the first hired employee at **PJ TRAILERS**. He was a young man of only 18 years. But Peter recognized something in Robert that he admired. Robert had a creative gift and Peter was willing to reward him for it.

This was a strength that Peter had. He knew his own limitations but he also knew he could hire employees who could do things he could not do. In Peter's mind, the problem was seldom bad employees; it was good employees, trying to do the wrong task.

Peter liked to empower his employees. He looked at each of them as a manager; managing his or her own time. The first thing Peter looked at before promoting someone was that person's time management habits. Did they show up on time at work and did they keep their word?

"Work hard and pay well" was Peter's motto. Ask Peter how long it took to build the first **PJ Trailer** and he will tell you. It may have taken a week, but he had kept track of the time. That same principle applied when **PJ Trailers** were coming off the assembly line at a rate of a trailer every seven minutes.

PJ Trailers assembly crews worked as a team in eight hour shifts. Working around the clock, the teams were in friendly competition. Employees worked for an hourly wage with a per unit bonus, paid to each team. The team with the highest production got the biggest bonus. That is why Peter knew how many minutes it took to assemble a **PJ Trailer.**

One of Peter's top managers was Roger. A hard working conscientious guy, he could be trusted with any task and it would be completed. He also came from a very conservative Mennonite background. He was aware that **PJ Trailers** was very profitable, and it bothered him.

To him, wanting to make more money was the equivalent of greed and that was wrong. To Peter, making money was good; it was the love of money that was wrong. Peter wanted to reward Roger for his faithful work habit and came up with a rather unique way of doing it.

The end of another year was coming and the company had shown a good profit. Peter knew Roger needed a new vehicle. He went to Paris, Texas and bought a brand new truck.

He took it over to Roger's house and gave the keys to Roger's wife. The next morning was Christmas. What a wonderful surprise when she handed Roger the keys to the truck.

Roger did not believe in Santa Claus, but he knew his boss, Peter Thiessen had a big heart. The truck he had just received was a bonus from **PJ Trailers** for a job well done. It may not have changed Roger's doctrine about money, but no doubt he enjoyed his new truck.

As the auditor had discovered in an earlier chapter, this was not the only time Peter Thiessen gave away pickup trucks as bonuses to productive and hard working supervisors. When it came to treating employees well, Peter Thiessen and PJ TRAILERS were the exception and not the rule.

One year PJ TRAILERS had done very well financially and was showing a good profit margin. Without a previous commitment or obligation, Peter Thiessen himself went to LOWRY CHEVROLET – CADILLAC in Paris, Texas. He purchased 14 new CHEVROLET, crew cab pickup trucks and gave one to each of the shift supervisors as a Christmas bonus.

Do you want loyal employees? Make sure the wives of employees are also treated well. That was another one of Peter Thiessen's convictions. Nothing demonstrated this better than providing good housing for families. Today many of the employees of PJ TRAILERS have purchased the manufactured homes made availble to them by PJ TRAILERS.

One other area that affected PJ TRAILERS employees was their spiritual life. Today there are five or more Mennonite churches in the Tigertown community. Peter Thiessen and PJ TRAILERS have been faithful supporters of most or all of these places of worship.

To Peter and Sara Thiessen, your spiritual life is a personal matter, but they will also be quick to tell you, "It is good to be involved in a local church." For that reason, Peter has personally helped to underwrite the financial cost for the construction of several Mennonite churches in the area.

The financial support of Peter and Sara Thiessen has not been limited to churches in the Mennonite communities. But that is where their roots are and they feel most comfortable.

Since the sale of PJ TRAILERS, Peter and Sara have had more time to travel. They have been to Africa and China, as well as Central and South America. Wherever they have gone, they always had an open checkbook.

Peter and Sara Thiessen believe what they have belongs to God. They are simply the caretakers and responsible for what they do with God's resources. Not always giving to every cause, they try to hear the voice of God and then do as they are lead to do.

No one person; one company or for that matter one church organization can fulfill the Great Commission Jesus gave, before going back to heaven. Going into all the world and preaching the Gospel to everyone is an assignment for the entire Church body, but there is an individual part each person can play.

Listen, Decide & Obey

Hear God's Voice - Confirm It - Then Do It

The business had been sold. They had a new home and several new vehicles. The funds from the sale of the business had been invested and there was money in the bank; now what? How about taking a trip to another country that is not doing as well as America or Canada or even Mexico?

That is what Peter and Sara Thiessen have done. In recent years they have made several of those visits to other countries, partly vacation, but mostly to help those who are less fortunate.

It was on a ministry trip to Mennonite colonies in Bolivia with Diedrich Harms, pastor of **LIGHTHOUSE MISSION CHURCH** in Tigertown, Texas that Peter first heard of a digital audio Bible on a handheld solar powered player.

Pastor Harms had brought it as a ministry tool. The device intrigued Peter but with his limited German schooling he had difficulty understanding it. Then he discovered the digital Bible was also available in his native Low German language.

Never one to do things in a small way, Peter instructed his executive assistant, Isaak Dyck to enquire about a getting volume discount on the purchase of a large quantity of players. As he expected, in lots of a thousand, the players were available at under half of the retail price and he placed an immediate order.

In addition to listening to the low German audio Bible daily, to date Peter has purchased and given away 1,250 of these audio Bibles in both the German, Low German and Spanish languages. As a side note, it is Peter's personal goal to listen to the entire New Testament, Matthew through Revelation, 50 times in this year.

Bolivia and Paraguay, like Mexico, were other countries where in times past, Mennonites had settled for the sake of their brand of "religious freedom." Located in the center of South America, they are both landlocked countries.

Just like they had done in Russia, in Canada and in Mexico, the Mennonites in South America had also settled in village communities. Although there was private ownership of property, still there was also a spirit of community.

It was in Paraguay where Peter met a couple who were facing a desperate need. In their good years, they had tried to farm and had managed to provide only the basic necessities to survive.

Now well past 40 years of age, the husband had fallen ill with a terminal disease. Peter could see that he was in the final stage of life and death seemed certain and close. Peter felt drawn to him and began asking him questions.

He discovered that the sick husband was so weary of life, he wanted to die. What seemed rather strange, he told Peter that he couldn't die. Apparently he was sick enough to die, but something was holding him back. Peter had met many sick people who wanted to live. But here was a man, who still could live many years, wanting to die.

At that point the wife of the man spoke up. She explained that they had spent all their cash resources on doctors and medicine, to no avail. They had gone so far as to sell their farm equipment and livestock to help pay for their medical bills. Now their very survival was threatened.

Normally when talking about spiritual matters, Peter can be somewhat shy, but suddenly he felt a supernatural boldness. "May I pray with you?" He asked the husband. "Please do," was his feeble reply. Peter knew that if this was not God's leading he was in deep trouble. As Peter began to pray, he paused.

There was something he had to ask the man. "Is there any unconfessed sin in your life, especially between you and your wife," he questioned? Now Peter felt awkward. What was that of his business? There was a moment of silence; then taking his wife's hand the man said, "Yes."

Peter did not need to know, nor did he want to know the details, but he had a sense that this was an issue of immoral behavior. Peter continued, "Confess your sin to God and to your wife privately. I know God will forgive you and I believe that with God's help, she will forgive you too."

He knew they needed time to be alone, so Peter excused himself. It wasn't long until Peter was asked to return to the side of the dying man. Peter could see there was a peace in the man's heart, he had not had before. At that moment, he had an idea. There was something that he could do to help them in their time of need.

Peter turned to the wife, who was sitting by her husband. "How much did you get for your farm equipment when you sold it?" He wanted to know. Hesitantly, she gave him the dollar amount. When Peter looked at it, he said, "Let me talk with my wife Sara when I get back to our home in Texas."

With her agreement, we will send you a check for the amount needed to buy back the livestock and farm equipment," When Peter returned to Tigertown, Texas, they kept their word. The amount can remain confidential, but it was more than a five figure amount.

The check in the form of a bank draft was sent to the couple in Paraguay. Then, just weeks later the news came; the man Peter had prayed for had passed away peacefully.

In 2010, travel took Peter Thiessen in another direction. This time he was going to the country of Ghana, on the continent of Africa. Sara was not able to go on this trip, so Isaak Dyck, his administrative executive assistant accompanied him.

Ghana has a population of about 23 million people and in the last year has been ranked as the fastest growing world economy with a growth rate of 20% in the year 2011. Peter loves travel and going to new places, but his real mission was to visit a young couple who had recently moved to Ghana.

Jake Reddekopp, born in Durango Mexico, grew up and lived in an Old Colony Mennonite community. In his early twenties he migrated to Ontario Canada. Through a series of unusual circumstances, Jake and Katherine Reddekopp felt the call to move to Ghana, Africa.

Their mission was threefold. They were going to help the Ghana natives how to become productive, modern farmers. Secondly, with Katherine's training in health care, they would help set up birthing centers for the delivery of babies. Thirdly, and really their highest goal; they would share the good news of the gospel with others who may not have heard it before.

Coming from the same Mennonite background in Mexico, Peter could relate to their vision. They were in need of a church building. All they needed was the finances for the construction and Peter wanted to help in that area.

They also talked about the need for farm equipment. Peter also had experience in that field, having bought and sold tractors and farm equipment as a business, both in Mexico and the US.

When Peter Thiessen and Isaak Dyck returned from Ghana, they began talking to others about the ministry of Jake and Katherine Reddekopp in Ghana.

Soon it was time to stop talking and start doing. Peter and some of his other church and business associates decided to send a container load of farm equipment to Ghana. A container is 40 feet long, 8 feet wide and 8 feet high and designed to be moved by truck, rail or ocean going vessel.

The load would include several tractors and other farm equipment that Jake could use in Ghana. When friends in Mexico heard about the planned shipment, they too wanted to have a part in it. Peter was there to see the equipment before it was loaded into the container.

Early in his career as a businessman, when Peter had faced an especially difficult financial situation, he had offered to give his **PJ TRAILER COMPANY** to God.

Peter Thiessen had told God that when he was able and had the opportunity to help others he would do it. He also promised to tell them it was God's money he was giving away. He was just the manager. These various undertakings are certainly evidence that Peter meant what he had said.

To God be the Glory

A Personal Word from Sara Thiessen

It was on a Saturday, in February of 2011 that we first met Peter and Dorothy Enns. This was not a planned event for any of us, but looking back we realize it also was not an accident. My husband, Peter and I both know it was a divine appointment.

We had never heard of them and they knew little or nothing about us. That afternoon as my husband began telling them the stories of how God had lead us, protected us and blessed our business, they seemed intrigued and we were glad they had come.

Thirty minutes into the **PJ Trailer** story, Peter Enns said, "Peter, this needs to be in a book." We had no idea Peter was a gifted author. He had not come looking for an assignment, but immediately we were comfortable with each other.

That night, Peter and Dorothy Enns and Bill and Helen Braun joined us in Paris, Texas. They came as our invited dinner guests. During the course of the evening, Peter Enns asked question after question and my husband Peter, kept on relating his unusual business experiences.

We invited our new friends to spend the night at our guest house and then join us for our church service the next morning. **Lighthouse Mission Church** in Tigertown, Texas was a new church in the area. Many of the members had come to Texas as employees of our company.

Our pastor, John Bergman had met Peter briefly the previous day. Both coming from a Mennonite background in Canada, they shared an immediate common bond. Although this was not the norm, the Pastor asked Peter to preach that Sunday morning.

Not knowing Peter Enns, we had no idea what to expect, but as he began to speak he had everyone's attention, including both children and adults. My husband Peter and I quickly recognized that this was not the first time he had preached in a church.

There was no doubt in our minds that Peter knew his Bible and his enthusiasm was contagious. We were amazed to learn that as a child, Peter had attended Sunday school at the Glencross **Evangelical Mennonite Mission Church** in Manitoba, one of our sister churches in Canada.

Several of the people attending the service that morning had lived within a mile of the home where Peter Enns had been raised as a lad.

It was hard to believe, but when we lived in Winkler, Manitoba, our home had been just a few houses down, from where Dorothy's parents lived.

Writing a book, or having a book written about both our Christian and business experience had been on our minds. But with our very limited education, this had seemed impossible. That morning, my husband called his executive assistant, Isaak Dyck and asked him to join us for lunch with our guests.

Adding Isaak and Tina Dyck to our table, gave them the opportunity to meet Peter and Dorothy one on one. Isaak and Tina felt like they had met a new "mom and dad." Later in the week, as we discussed the now "new book idea," Isaak felt confident that if there ever was going to be a book written about Peter Thiessen, Peter Enns was the right person to write it.

In 1973 Peter and Dorothy Enns had moved from Canada to Tulsa, Oklahoma. They lived just three hours away. We didn't know it, but it had been Peter's secret desire to visit some of the Mennonite colonies who had settled in Mexico in the 1920s.

Well, that is where both my husband and I were born and we still have business interests there. We were planning a business trip to Mexico so we invited Peter and Dorothy Enns to join us. If he was going to write a book about our life and our business related experiences, it certainly would be helpful for them to visit the country of our birth.

It was only a question of when we would make the trip. This was something they both wanted to do and it would give us time to really get to know one another. Soon we were on our way. Spending a week with someone you have just met can be a challenge, but this trip was a delight for all of us.

Going to the Mennonite villages in Mexico also gave Peter and Dorothy the opportunity to renew their Low German (Plautdietsch) language skills and something they both really seemed to enjoy.

It gave Peter and Dorothy a new insight into the lives of the Mennonites still living in Mexico. It was a busy week as we visited village after village, including the very homes where Peter and I were born and raised.

Dorothy and I felt comfortable with each other. I hadn't laughed so much in years. We joked about being sisters who had been adopted and didn't know it. Peter and Peter enjoyed playing one-upmanship; one asking questions and the other trying to come up with reasonable answers.

When we returned home all of us knew that writing the book was a good idea. We had agreed on the book title. It would be called **Blessed to be a Blessing,** with a subtitle, **How to do Business God's Way.**

We gave Peter Enns permission to ask any questions and promised to provide honest answers. Our children had been a part of our business and we wanted them to be part of the book as well. We encouraged Peter and Dorothy to meet individually with our family members and verify some of the hard to believe stories we had shared.

Having a book written about a person's life is a humbling experience. You wonder, "What will people think?" "Does it sound like we are bragging?" "Is this really the way that it happened?" These and a host of other questions have flooded our minds. Still, as my husband Peter and I talked about it, we knew this is something that we wanted to do.

Peter and Dorothy had heard about our grandson Elijah and his heart transplant ordeal. Seeing the story in the Paris News, they were both in tears as they read about the mother, Mary Jane who donated the heart of her son, Matthew so that our grandson Elijah could live.

Sitting at the breakfast table one morning, Dorothy said; "The story of Elijah and his heart transplant could be in a book by itself." Without another word, Peter left the table and returned a few minutes later with a title and cover layout for another book, **"Love is in the Heart."**

They didn't know it, but our daughter Sarah, the mother of little Elijah, had just talked to her father and me, about the possibility of Peter Enns doing a special book about the heart transplant story.

A few days later when Peter and Dorothy came to visit and showed us the title and cover design, it was a confirmation to us. When Henry and Sarah Friesen and the rest of our family heard about the book idea, there was a unanimous, "Yes."

Here is where sweet becomes bitter. In July of 2011, Elijah had to undergo a routine checkup on his heart. Everything seemed normal, but then complications set in. Just minutes after, coming out of the anesthesia, Elijah passed away.

About six weeks after Elijah's funeral, Peter and Dorothy Enns came to visit our family. They asked Henry and Sarah if the book about Elijah was still in their plans. Without any hesitation they said, "Yes," and we as grandparents agreed.

Before he passed away, Elijah had been aware that a book was being written about him and his heart transplant. Obviously there was much he did not understand but still he was excited about it.

Both Henry and Sarah Friesen and Mary Jane Liles Sauseda want to continue in their commitment to help create organ transplant donor awareness, especially for children.

It is their intent that as they tell their story of what they lived through, other people will also catch the vision of becoming an organ donor. There is so much to learn about giving the gift of life to someone else who is waiting for an organ transplant.

It is also their desire that other hurting families, who are going through difficult health challenges will be encouraged to trust God, no matter of the outcome, because God is a good God. Even when we don't feel it, He is there all the time.

Make-A-Wish

A Final Farewell to Elijah

THE MAKE-A-WISH FOUNDATION is a non-profit organization in the United States that grants wishes to children (two and a half to eighteen years old) who have life-threatening medical conditions. Elijah Friesen, Peter Thiessen's six year old grandson was on that list.

Because of his serious heart condition, he had been on the MAKE-A-WISH list for over a year. Following his heart transplant Elijah was granted his wish of a lifetime. It had been to visit DISNEY WORLD in Florida and meet his favorite Disney characters.

In July of 2011, the MAKE-A-WISH FOUNDATION, made Elijah's wish became a reality, as he and his little sister Kezia and their parents, Henry and Sarah Friesen boarded the flight headed for DISNEY WORLD. The experience was more than anyone could have wished for, as DISNEY WORLD rolled out the red carpet for Elijah and his family.

After a two week stay in Florida, the Friesen family returned to Texas with great memories and photos of a vacation they would never forget. For Elijah it had truly been "A dream come true." Before his heart transplant he had not been able to enjoy the sheer pleasure of being alive. In the past days he had lived life to the full.

They had returned from their trip on Saturday. The following Tuesday Elijah was scheduled to be back at the clinic in Dallas for a routine "heart transplant" checkup. Following the biopsy procedure, as he was recovering from the anesthesia, complications began to develop and his parents knew there was a problem.

It was only a matter of minutes until they heard the sad news from the Doctor, that Elijah's heart had stopped beating and he had passed away. Peter and Sara Thiessen were on their way to Canada, when the cell phone rang and they learned what had just happened to their little grandson.

As the word spread, soon other family members who had been in Canada, gathered at the Grand Forks, North Dakota airport. Peter Thiessen had chartered two private jet airplanes to take them back to Paris, Texas. There was little conversation on the flight, but everyone knew that Henry and Sarah Friesen needed them.

The following Saturday the **Lighthouse Mission Church** at Tigertown, Texas was filled to capacity as friends came to say their final farewell to Elijah. Tears flowed freely, as young cousins sang and shared memories of their little friend.

Mary Jane Liles Sauseda, the mother who had donated the heart of her late son Matthew, had come to the memorial service. As she spoke to those in attendance and embraced Elijah's mother, Sarah knew that Mary Jane truly understood what she and Henry were going through in the loss of their precious little boy.

One of the doctor's who had been involved with Elijah's heart transplant was also present. As she commented on her experience with Elijah, there was no doubt that he had been more than another patient. Elijah had become her special friend. Addressing

Mary Jane, the mother who gave Elijah his new heart, she said, "Mary Jane, you are my hero."

Pastor Harms was brief in his comments. There are times in life when no one really has an answer as to why certain things happen, and this was one of those times. But being people of faith, the Pastor spoke confidently of a day of resurrection when we will see our loved ones again.

Building a successful business has always been a priority to Peter Thiessen. But something of greater importance was imparting faith to his family. Losing his young grandson had been a tearful experience, but there were also tears of joy as Peter watched his children, standing together, strong in faith, trusting God in this most difficult time in their lives.

Doing Business God's Way
You Can Do it Too!

D OING BUSINESS GOD'S WAY is not limited to a few
special people. It is God's desire for every man or woman
who is in business. Peter Thiessen's story is simply an example of
what God has done for an ordinary individual who was willing to
partner with Him.

Why not take God as your business partner? It is not a question
of being good enough, or religious enough. It is a matter of being
honest with God and being willing to take Him at his word. The
Bible calls that "Walking by faith." At the risk of sounding preachy,
the Bible says that, "Without faith it is impossible to please God"
(Hebrews 11:6).

Like Peter Thiessen discovered, God makes a great partner
in business. He has unlimited resources, He is all wise and even
knows the future. In addition, God has the ability to give you favor
with others and can even make your enemies be at peace with you.

The Bible is loaded with wisdom principles for those who are in business. Just like Peter Thiessen did, in the opening chapter of this book, the scriptures invite us to come and ask God for wisdom. What God did for Peter, he will do for anyone else. God is not a respecter of persons. However he will do it in His own way and at the right time.

Are you ready to start **Doing Business God's Way?** It begins with having a personal relationship with God. He is our Creator and He also wants to be our Father.

Becoming a Son or Daughter of God takes a simple step of faith. That means taking God at his Word. The best known scripture in the Bible (John 3:16) capsulizes God's plan for us.

It says, "For God so loved the world that He gave His only begotten Son, that whoever believes on Him should not perish, but have everlasting life."

Three Steps To Developing
A Personal Relationship With God.

The first step in having a personal relationship with God is to recognize that because of Adam's disobedience, we are all part of a fallen human race and are sinners by nature. Romans 3:23 puts it this way, "All have sinned and come short of the glory of God."

The second step is to realize that Jesus, born of the Virgin Mary, was the perfect Lamb of God, who came to take away the sins of the world. He died! His blood paid the penalty for the sins of the world, and then He rose again.

Today, He sits at the right hand of the Father. He has all power! He was given a Name that is above every Name; that at the Name of Jesus every knee should bow and every tongue confess that Jesus Christ is Lord.

The third step is to invite God into your life and make him your partner for eternity. Before Jesus went to the cross, He made this statement in John chapter 14. He said, "I go to prepare a place for you, and I will come again and receive you unto myself, that where I am you may be also." What a great promise. Welcome to the family!

Not only does the Bible contain wonderful business principles, it also has many promises of God's intended blessing for each of His children. This book, **Blessed to be a Blessing,** is based on one of those promises.

Speaking to Abraham in Genesis 12:2 God said, "I will bless you . . . . and you shall be a blessing." When we believe God and take Him at his Word, we become a part of Abraham's family and heirs to the promises God made to him.

In Deuteronomy 8, the Bible makes another statement. It says, "It is God who gives us the power to get wealth, that He may establish His covenant." Feeding the hungry, helping the needy and taking the good news of the gospel to the world, all takes money. **Doing business God's way** is part of the answer to meeting these needs.

Having a personal relationship with God, means that we can talk to Him, and He talks to us. We can speak to God in prayer and He will speak to us through the Word of God.

He can also speak to us in our heart and mind, as well as through other people. One of the most important things we have to do is to learn to be a good listener.

The scriptures teach us that as human beings, we were created in the image of God. In Jeremiah 1: 5 God says that while we were still in our mother's womb He knew us. He goes on to say that each one of us was set apart for a special purpose by our Creator.

Everything ever invented or created by an inventor was created and designed for a definite purpose and to fill a specific need. Certainly, when an all wise God created us, He also had a purpose in mind. Discovering God's purpose for our life is the beginning of **"Doing Business God's Way."**

The first step in finding your purpose in life is to simply ask God what He wants you to do. He knows your potential and what will ultimately fulfill your mission. That is a truth everyone who wants to **"DO BUSINESS GOD'S WAY"** needs to realize and accept.

Secondly, start doing something that fills a need in the life of another person. The old saying, "Find a need and fill it," is still true today. There is a task, an assignment, a need that only you can fill in your own unique way.

Doing something you have never done before certainly is risky business. Will you succeed or fail? Only God knows. Whatever the outcome, God will be with you. Should you fail, God will give you strength to try again.

The next time you will be wiser and stronger and the victory will be even greater. When you succeed, and that is God's desire for you, give Him the credit. Always remember, it is God who gives us the power to get wealth, that He may establish his covenant with us. Timing is very important and "Nothing is as powerful as an idea whose time has come."

So what should you believe God for? How big should you dream? That is up to you. The Bible is full of stories of ordinary people who took God at His word and did the impossible. A good rule to follow is: "Dream big, but begin small." Even baby elephants begin with a single cell in the mother's womb.

Some of the more humorous stories in the Bible deal with older folks, who could already have been in retirement. Zacharias, the father of John the Baptist was one of those delightful characters.

From the tribe of Levi, he was a good, old man and had a good, old wife. He was doing his priestly duties at the temple, when he heard someone calling his name.

It was God's messenger angel, named Gabriel. "Fear not," the angel began. "God has heard your prayers." You can almost hear Zacharias asking, "What prayers?" "The one about the baby" the angel continued.

Zacharias may well have responded with a surprising answer, "That was fifty years ago." Then Gabriel would explain that he knew that. Gabriel then told Zacharias to go and tell Elizabeth that she was going to have a baby.

Obviously, like most every other young couple, when Zacharias and his wife had first married, they desired to have a baby. According to the Bible, Elizabeth was barren and unable to have any children.

As people of faith, they prayed and asked God for a child, but for whatever reason the prayer went unanswered. Now that they were both old, the miracle happens and we know the rest of the story and their miracle son, John the Baptist.

The baby was born and was the physical cousin of Jesus, the Christ. He grew up to become a great preacher. Yes, God had heard the prayer of Zacharias and Elizabeth when they were young and answered it when they were both old. Remember, it's never too late for God to do what He has called you to do..

The stories in this book are true. Peter Thiessen is a simple, but a gifted man. With little formal education, he dared to believe that he could do what he was created to do. In the process he built a sizeable business. He knows he could not have done it by himself.

Peter is quick to say that God is the source of his success. But he also knows he had many other gifted people who worked with him. Most importantly, Peter had Sara, his wife, who believed in God and in Peter. She stood with Peter through the bad times and the good. Today, after many years she is still there as his friend and business partner.

Don't start building a trailer factory, unless God tells you to do it. Know that with God, nothing is impossible. If you can believe it, God can and will help you make it happen. Learn to hear God's voice by taking time to listen and then acting on his Word.

It is important to believe in God. Most everyone does. But it is also important to believe in yourself and in what God says about you. In the Bible, in the book of Numbers, we read a most fascinating story. Under the capable leadership of Moses, the Children of Israel have come out of Egypt and are on their way to the Promised Land of Israel.

Two million strong, they stood at the border, ready to enter their new territory. Moses decided to send 12 men to go in and spy out the land. After 40 days they returned with a glowing report. "The land is as we were told," they began, "but there are giants in the land." The ten spies continued; "We were like grasshoppers in their sight."

"Don't go into the land because we are not able to possess it," was their closing statement. However, two of the twelve, Joshua and Caleb said, "Let's go in at once for we are well able." They knew that God was on their side.

The multitude of people believed the negative report of the majority and spent the next 40 years going in circles in the desert. Will you listen to the ten or will you partner with the two? Like the Children of Israel, we have a choice to make.

Here is what God says about you in Jeremiah 1:5, "I knew you before I formed you in your mother's womb." He knows you better than you know yourself.

You have abilities and strengths that he placed in you, for such a time as this. Avoid the influence of those who would tear you down or belittle what you desire to do.

The Bible is full of heroes of faith who did great things for God, but there are also stories of people, who after they had great successes, messed up in life.

Men like David and Samson and even Solomon who wrote the book on wisdom. However, even after they failed, when they repented, God still blessed them in what they did for the kingdom of God.

In Deuteronomy chapter 8, (NKJV) God promises to bless his people. But with the promise comes a special warning not to forget God when we experience material blessings and financial success in life. Here is what it says:

6) "Therefore you shall keep the commandments of the LORD your God, to walk in His ways and to fear Him.

7) For the LORD your God is bringing you into a good land, a land of brooks of water, of fountains and springs, that flow out of valleys and hills;

8) a land of wheat and barley, of vines and fig trees and pomegranates, a land of olive oil and honey;

9) a land in which you will eat bread without scarcity, in which you will lack nothing; a land whose stones are iron and out of whose hills you can dig copper.

10) When you have eaten and are full, then you shall bless the LORD your God for the good land which He has given you.

11) Beware that you do not forget the LORD your God by not keeping His commandments, His judgments, and His statutes which I command you today,

12) lest—when you have eaten and are full, and have built beautiful houses and dwell in them;

13) and when your herds and your flocks multiply, and your silver and your gold are multiplied, and all that you have is multiplied;

14) when your heart is lifted up, and you forget the LORD your God who brought you out of the land of Egypt, from the house of bondage; 15) who led you through that great and terrible wilderness, in which were fiery serpents and scorpions and thirsty land where there was no water; who brought water for you out of the flinty rock;

16) who fed you in the wilderness with manna, which your fathers did not know, that He might humble you and that He might test you, to do you good in the end,

17) then you say in your heart, 'My power and the might of my hand have gained me this wealth.'

18) And you shall remember the LORD your God, for it is He who gives you power to get wealth, that He may establish His covenant which He swore to your fathers, as it is this day.

Peter Thiessen's life and the experiences related in this book are a testimony that God keeps His Word. When you recognize your calling in life and commit yourself to walk in obedience to His Word you too can expect to enjoy God's blessing.

Another thing Peter emphasizes is the importance of praying for our national leaders. He has made it a practice to pray for the President of the United States by name daily and encourages others to do the same. He prays for Godly wisdom for the President, in decisions and asks God for divine protection for the first family.

If the message in this book has blessed you, Peter Thiessen would like to hear from you. For his contact information go online to: www.goodwordinternational.com

Kind Words from Friends
Money Can Buy Influence but Not Friendship

Peter Thiessen has had the experience of building a business beyond his wildest dreams. The **PJ TRAILERS** manufacturing plant two miles west of Tigertown, Texas stands as a testimony of what can happen when an ordinary person discovers his or her life's purpose; puts their faith in God and works hard at his or her chosen calling.

In the process of building a successful business, there is the temptation of putting money and things above people. In our competitive world keeping a win/win attitude is not always easy. It would be an overstatement to say that everyone who knows Peter Thiessen speaks only well of him. But here are several of his business acquaintances who chose to put their thoughts and feelings on paper.

Isaac Thiessen
Tex-Star Windows - President
1085 US 180 W. Seminole, TX 79360

Peter Thiessen is my older brother. He may not be a tall man, but he has always been a big brother to me. As part of the family, I can assure you that Peter is not perfect, but he is a man who has faith in God as well as in other people.

I recall when I was just a lad of 14 and Peter made me his business partner. At the time he was importing farm equipment into Mexico, from the United States. At that very young age, he trusted me with thousands of dollars.

One particular event stands out in my mind. It had been a good week and I had made equipment sales of over $60,000 Pesos. I had no safe place to keep the money, so I put it into my cowboy boots. I walked around with all that cash in my boots until the bank opened on Monday morning.

Years later when **PJ Trailers** set up their factory in Mexico, I had the opportunity of working with my brother Peter again. Working with family members is not always easy and we have had our misunderstandings. But we have both learned, good relationships are more important than money.

Peter is never a small thinker and the time we spent together at **PJ Trailers**, helped me grow in my thinking. In 2009, when we decided to start **Tex-Star Windows** in Seminole, Texas, Peter was there to help me, his younger brother, with good advice for building a successful company.

I love my brother and I am pleased that in this book Peter is giving God the glory for what he has been able to accomplish.

ERNIE KEHLER,
GREENVALLEY EQUIPMENT INC., - PRESIDENT
MORDEN, MANITOBA, CANADA

I have had the pleasure of knowing Peter Thiessen, the founder of **PJ TRAILERS**, for more than 25 years. From my perspective, as an farm equipment dealer as well as a personal friend, over the years Peter and I have enjoyed a mutually rewarding relationship.

When Peter Thiessen moved to Tigertown, Texas in 1989 and started his **PJ TRAILER MANUFACTURING BUSINESS** we were his first Canadian dealer. Being a distributor of **PJ TRAILERS** was a profitable business experience.

His business philosophy always was, "Volume." Peter used to say, "I would rather sell in volume and make a little profit opposed to making a big profit with a little volume."

Peter always appreciated his family. Working together with his children as a team, they helped him to become one of the largest manufacturers of trailers in North America.

Knowing Peter like I do, I am sure that selling **PJ TRAILERS** is not the end of Peter Thiessen's business ventures. No doubt there will be other business opportunities in his future.

His faith in the Lord has been very evident in building and growing the **PJ TRAILER MANUFACTURING COMPANY** to the level it has become.

The true story of Peter's life, including both his failures as well as his successes, proves that honesty, hard work, and faith can help to build a successful business.

Henry Penner,
Little Morden Service - President
Morden, Manitoba, Canada

My business relationship with Peter Thiessen began in 1979. I was one of the first customers to purchase some of his **Air Tank Bumpers**. That was only the beginning of our business dealings.

Then In 1981 Peter bought a truckload of knives and hand tools from us and hauled them to Mexico and resold them.

Several years later Peter Thiessen purchased the property on Highway 14, between Winkler and Morden, Manitoba from us. It is the current **PJ Canada**, office. I still recall when we made the deal; we took several **PJ trailers** in trade, as part payment for the property purchase.

In the years that followed, we have had numerous other business transactions with Peter Thiessen. A man of his word, it has always been a pleasure doing business with him.

Dale R Gislason
Fellow of the Certified
General Accountant Association
Senior Partner Gislason, Targownik, Peters
Winkler, Manitoba, Canada

Our firm has served as external accountants and auditors for more than twenty years to the various businesses that Peter Thiessen has established in Canada and today we are still engaged in that capacity.

I personally know his story to be one of courage, perseverance and faith. From humble beginnings in the early 1980s, Peter, together with his partners and family, built multiple companies.

There are numerous lessons for all entrepreneurs in Peter's business life. Through good times and bad, he adapted to changes in markets and economic conditions, in pursuit of business success.

Although he encountered many difficulties and setbacks along the way, Peter persevered and ultimately realized his dreams with **PJ Trailers** in Tigertown, Texas.

Working alongside with his family, their efforts culminated in creating a major manufacturing operation that still today, has a significant presence in the United States, in Mexico and in the Canadian marketplace.

Along the way Peter learned how to rely on others and reaffirmed the important things in life. Beginning with his own family members, he surrounded himself with people who had the skills his business needed.

Peter's business achievement is a testament to the old adage that "To truly succeed you must first fail." The ability to learn from mistakes, to regroup and adapt to change, are key ingredients in the recipe for building a profitable owner managed business.

Peter has demonstrated that even in our high tech world, the entrepreneurial spirit is still alive and well and can compete in global markets.

George Fehr
Lamar Trailers - Founder & President
Maxey, Texas

In 1994 we were living in Seminole, Texas. Born in a Mennonite community in Mexico, we had come to the United States and had Immigration Green Card status. Like Peter, I too had very limited education and had attended only our Church School in Mexico.

We had heard about Peter Thiessen and **PJ Trailers** in Tigertown, Texas and I decided to give him a call. Although I was not a welder, I was a hard worker and Peter agreed to give me a job.

We arrived in Tigertown, Texas, with our clothes on our back and everything else that we owned, packed inside our car. I started working at **PJ Trailers** at minimum wage.

In the eight years I worked for **PJ Trailers**, I quickly learned the trade and became a shop foreman. I was one of the guys mentioned earlier in this book, who received a new pickup truck as a year-end bonus.

My experience at **PJ Trailers** gave me both the skill and the confidence to begin **Lamar Trailers**. Although we became direct competitors to **PJ Trailers**, through the years, Peter Thiessen and I have remained good friends.

Thanks to Peter Thiessen for giving me the opportunity to work in his Company, and his entrepreneurial role model I have been able to follow. Today we employ 43 people at our **Lamar Trailer Factory,** in Maxey, Texas.

John Dyck
Delco Trailer - Founder & President
Sumner, Texas

Peter Thiessen is my friend. He has a good heart for people. Peter was there for me when I needed help.

We had moved to Tigertown, Texas with the intent of starting a trailer manufacturer company. After working in the trailer industry, in 2006 I decided to start my own trailer company; **Delco Trailers.**

We began building cattle trailers and did not want to be in direct competition with **PJ Trailers.**

Shortly after we started the Company, I knew we did not have the financial capital that we needed to build the Company, so I went to see Peter Thiessen.

I asked him to consider becoming a partner with me. Out of the kindness of his heart he agreed and invested substantially in our Company to help us.

The past number of years have been very good for us. After the sale of **PJ Trailers** in 2008, we have been able to become the sole owners of **Delco Trailers.**

I will be forever grateful to Peter Thiessen and the faith he had in me as a young businessman, to help me start our Company. He is definitely one of a kind.

George Loewen
President, UMC Logistic
Seminole, Texas & Cuauhtémoc, Mexico

I was a "one man/one truck operation," transporting used farm equipment from both the US and Canada to Mexico. When **PJ Trailers,** began building trailers in Cuauhtémoc, Mexico, I asked Peter Thiessen, who also happened to be my brother-in-law, who would transport the finished trailers back to the USA and Canada?

Always quick to make a decision, Peter and his brothers who were involved with **PJ Trailers,** offered me the opportunity to deliver their trailers. As a result I have been able to also build an international trucking company.

Starting in 1998, with a letter of guaranteed business from **PJ Trailers** I began **UMC Logistics.** Our new company grew very quickly. With the increased business coming from **PJ Trailers,** we were able to purchase additional trucks and flat bed trailers.

At the peak of our business, before **PJ Trailers** was sold in 2008, we had as many as 22 **Transport Tractors** on the road. Still today, we have 16 **Kenwood Tractors** and employ 17 full time drivers.

I know, beyond any doubt; had Peter Thiessen not given me the encouragement and the opportunity to build my company, today I would still be a "one truck operation." "Thank you Peter for the faith you had in me."

Diedrich Harms, Pastor
Lighthouse Mission Church
Tigertown, Texas

Peter Thiessen and I have known each other since we were just boys, growing up together in Mexico. During the last four years I have had the opportunity to travel extensively with him on various missions' related assignments.

Spending time together on these lengthy trips, Peter and I got to know each other on a much deeper level. Watching him, I have come to realize that he is a very generous man, who delights in giving of his resources wherever and whenever he sees a need that he can fill.

There are several outstanding concepts that I have seen in Peter. (1) He has an optimistic outlook on life. (2) He has an amazing capacity to remember things. (3) He is willing to accept what he cannot change. (4) He readily admits when he sees that he is wrong.

In my opinion, what has helped to make Peter so successful in business is his strong faith in God and the willingness to act on God's promises.

He has an uncanny ability for making decisions, as well as a spirit of discernment. Peter is straightforward and acts on his convictions. Whatever he promises, he tries to fulfill.

Philipp R. Ens
Chairman, Triple E Canada Ltd.
Winkler Manitoba, Canada

In spite of his academic limitations, Peter Thiessen has forged ahead to build a business that ranks as one of the great entrepreneurial success stories of our day.

He has thrived, when many others who watched him, thought he was doomed to fail. In the face of problems such as fires, financial difficulties, and unreasonably high interest rates, he kept on going.

It was an inspiration to witness Peter's ability to source supplies from off shore and to collect deposits on products that were not yet manufactured.

He was able to rally his work force when funds were in short supply, and he grew to understand the larger scope of a manufacturing operation like **PJ Trailers.**

One of Peter's companies in Winkler, Manitoba, Canada was named **Allstar Manufacturing.** Little did he, or anyone else at the time, realize that Peter Thiessen was the number one star.

Through it all, I have watched Peter in both good and in bad times. He maintained his faith in God and in himself and was confident that he would ultimately achieve success in the highly competitive world of business.

Although **PJ Trailers** now is under new ownership, the Company in Tigertown, Texas still stands as a monument to the perseverance and integrity of Peter Thiessen.

DOUG CLARK
PRESIDENT/CEO - PJ TRAILERS MFG CO. INC.
TIGERTOWN, TEXAS

Peter Thiessen is a perfect example of an American success story. It was no accident that **PJ TRAILERS** has become synonymous with high quality and great customer service in the American trailer industry.

From its beginnings, Peter was committed to building a product that was second to none in terms of quality. Because Peter was the one delivering trailers to dealers at the beginning, he was able to communicate with dealers and make changes and product modifications to assure **PJ TRAILERS** success.

PJ TRAILERS success is directly attributable to the quality and craftsmanship Peter was determined to keep in every trailer manufactured by the Company.

During periods where competitors were cutting product quality to maintain profit margins, Peter was able to lead changes in the manufacturing process to help reduce production costs, avoiding the loss of quality that many of his competitors were forced to make.

It was no accident that **PJ TRAILERS** grew to become one of the leading trailer manufacturers in North America. It was hard work and determination.

That is the ongoing legacy Peter Thiessen has left in the employees who today, continue to produce that same high quality of craftsmanship and customer service, as Peter did 20 years ago when he began building trailers and growing the **PJ TRAILER COMPANY.**